Prince William County Virginia

Will Book "C"

- 1734-1744 -

Compiled by:
John Frederick Dorman

Southern Historical Press, inc.
Greenville, South Carolina

This volume was reproduced
from a personal copy located in
the Publishers private library

Please direct all correspondence and book orders to:
SOUTHERN HISTORICAL PRESS, Inc.
1071 Park West Blvd.
Greenville, SC   29611

Copyright By: John Frederick Dorman 1956
ISBN #978-1-63914-334-4
Printed in the United States of America

To

Earl Gregg Swem, Litt.D., LL.D.

in gratitude for

his advice and encouragement

Preface

Prince William County, Virginia, was created by an Act of the Assembly of May, 1730, from the upper parts of King George and Stafford counties. Its territory comprised "... all the land, on the heads of the said counties, above Chopwansick Creek, on Potomack river, and Deep run, on Rappahannock river, and a south-west line to be made, from the head of the north branch of the said creek, to the head of the said Deep run ..." and included the present counties of Prince William, Fairfax, Fauquier, Loudoun and Arlington. This act became effective on 26 March 1731. (Hening, Statutes at Large, v. 4, p. 303.)

The county was named for William Augustus, Duke of Cumberland, one of the sons of King George II.

Will Book C is the only colonial will book remaining for Prince William County. Whether it is the earliest will book has not been determined, but it is probable that more than the one will, three inventories and one estate account, which were contained in the missing six pages of this book, were presented to the Court between March, 1731, and September, 1734. If so, the volume or volumes in which they were recorded have suffered the same fate as the will books of the 1750's and '60's which are missing.

The earliest records in this volume are attested by John Gregg, Deputy Clerk. Catesby Cooke, the Clerk, signed the records entered between 20 November 1734 and 22 November 1742. Upon the creation of Fairfax County he relinquished the office and was succeeded by P. Wagener, who signed the records from 24 January 1742/3 through the end of the volume.

The county was virtually cut in half in 1742 by the Act of the Assembly creating Fairfax County, which included the area of present Fairfax, Loudoun and Arlington counties along the Potomac River. (Hening, v. 5, pp. 207-08.)

The first county seat of Prince William was on Occoquan Creek but in 1742 it was moved to a point on Cedar Run.

There were two parishes in Prince William County during the period covered by this volume. Hamilton Parish was formed 1 January 1731 from Overwharton Parish, Stafford County. After 1 November 1732 that portion of Hamilton north of Occoquan Creek became Truro Parish and the part of Hanover Parish, King George County, which lay in Prince William County was then added to Hamilton. In 1742 Truro fell into Fairfax County.

Although many of the early records of Prince William County are now gone, some of the original papers which were recorded in Will Book C have been returned to the State of Virginia. These papers, including several original wills, are now preserved in the Manuscripts Department of the

Library of the College of William and Mary at Williamsburg, a state institution, where they have been arranged and inventoried so that the contents are accessible to the public. The original papers of the following records from Will Book C are the only ones which have been preserved. The College of William and Mary does not have any other Prince William County records.

Bronaugh, Samuel	Estate account (pp. 431-32)
Farrow, Abram	Will (pp. 443-44)
	Executor's bond (pp. 444-46)
Fegan, Edward	Administrator's bond (pp. 439-41)
Filkins, Henry	Inventory (pp. 419-20)
French, James	Will (pp. 421-23)
	Administrator's bond (pp. 423-24)
	Inventory (pp. 425-27)
	Division (pp. 446-47)
Gregg, John	Will (pp. 404-06)
	Executrix's bond (pp. 406-07)
Grinan, Owin	Administrator's bond (p. 447)
Lawson, Marmaduke	Will (pp. 407-08)
	Executor's bond (pp. 408-09)
	Inventory (pp. 417-19)
McDowel, Thomas	Will (p. 351)
McKenzey, Daniel	Administrator's bond (pp. 427-28)
	Inventory (pp. 430-31)
Morris, Ann	Will (pp. 429-30)
Osborn, Thomas	Estate account (pp. 428-29)
Smith, Thomas	Administratrix's bond (pp. 438-39)
Spicer, Rosser	Administrator's bond (pp. 441-43)
Steward, William	Inventory (p. 355)
Sute, Edward	Inventory (pp. 396-97)
Taylor, Charles	Estate account (p. 400)
Tebbs, Daniel	Will (pp. 358-59)
	Inventory (pp. 412-13)
Thornberry, Richard	Administratrix's bond (pp. 403-04)
	Inventory (p. 410)
Wallis, Thomas	Inventory (pp. 400-01)
Williams, David	Administrator's bond (pp. 411-12)
	Inventory (p. 421)
Young, Edward	Inventory (p. 424)
	Estate account (pp. 424-25)
Young, Thomas	Guardian's bond (p. 409)

The abstracts in this volume of these thirty-six records combine the reading of the original paper and the recorded copy. They are generally faithful to the spelling of the original wherever there are differences. An exact transcription of the records has not been possible in this book of abstracts but close conformity to the original wording and form has been attempted. The misspelling of appraisement was particularly frequent.

Wherever a mark rather than a signature was affixed, the mark has been placed in parentheses. An "X" has been used not only for that symbol but also for a cross and for any other symbol which cannot be reproduced on a typewriter. An "I" has been used in those instances in which, although a "J" was obviously intended, the mark appears more like a modern "I". Parentheses without a mark inclosed are used in those instances in which the words "his mark" appeared without an accompanying mark.

Since this book covers a period prior to the change of the calendar, the dates in January, February and most of March must be altered to the succeeding year. The dates are copied as they appeared in the will book, but the correct year date according to modern reckoning is given at the head of each page.

The names have been indexed under the spelling most frequently used in this volume, with the variations indicated. No attempt has been made to conform the spelling to later use or even to the usage most common in the 1730's and '40's although it is hoped that the cross references in the index assist in locating any name.

Since the first abstracts of records in Will Book C were made the volume has been treated for lasting preservation and it now bears a page recording that it was "Restored in honor of Mrs. Wade Hampton Ellis (Dessie Corwin Chase), 3rd Vice Directress, by Washington Branch, Association for the Preservation of Virginia Antiquities, 1955."

My thanks are due Mr. Worth H. Storke, Clerk of Prince William County, and the assistants in his office for their kindness and friendliness during my visits to Manassas, and to my many friends at the Library of the College of William and Mary.

John Frederick Dorman

2311 Connecticut Avenue, N. W.
Washington, D. C.
22 April 1956

Prince William County, Virginia
Will Book C
1734 - 1744

The first six pages of this volume are missing. The index shows that the contents were:

Page 1. Linton, Margaret's Inventory
Page 2. Quarles, Moses's Inventory
Page 4. Bivens, Thomas's Inventory
Page 5. Bivens, Mary's Account agt. Thoms. Bivens Estate
Page 5. Russell, Nathl's Will
Page 6. Gibson, Jacob et al Bond

Page 7. Remaining portion of the above mentioned administrator's bond. [Signed by] Jacob Gibson
Morris (M V) Veal
John (I) Johnson
Wit: J. Estace, John Gregg
18 Sept. 1734. Ack. and OR.

Pages 7-8. Inventory of estate of Wm. Markham, dec., made in obedience to order of 21 Aug. 1734.
Total valuation ₤ 37.4.0.
[Appraisers] Tho. (T) Ashbe
Ralph (R H) Huse
John Hardin
Elizab. (E) Markham, extx., signed the inventory
18 Sept. 1734. Elizabeth Markham, executrix of William Markham, dec., returned this inventory and appraisement which was OR.

Pages 8-11. Inventory of estate of Charles Broadwater, dec., made in obedience to order of 21 Aug. 1734. Appraisers sworn before John Collvil.
Includes 16 negroes at ₤ 211. No total valuation given.
Thos. Lewis
Thos. Smith
Michael Ashford
18 Sept. 1734. Hugh West, admr. with the will annexed of Charles Broadwater, dec., returned this inventory and appraisement which was OR.

Page 12. Inventory of the estate of John Tillett, dec.
Total valuation ₤ 31.4.3.
Thos. Ford
William (M) Simson
Richard (R) Simson
Appraisers sworn before Wm. Godfrey.
Morris Veale and John Turley, executors.
19 Sept. 1734. Morris Veale, one of the executors of John Tillett, dec., returned this inventory which was OR.

Pages 13-14. Bond of Margarit Russell, Morris Veal and John Johnson unto Thomas Harrison, justice. For ₤ 100. 20 Nov. 1734. Margaret Russell is admx. of Nathaniel Russell, dec.

Margaret (X) Russell
Morris (M) Veal
John (T) Johnson

Wit: R. Stan [Stace?]
20 Nov. 1734. Ack. and OR.

Pages 14-16. Bond of George Underwood, Thomas Ashby and Francis Searson unto Thomas Harrison, justice. For ₤20. 20 Nov. 1734. George Underwood is admr. of John Underwood, dec.

George (V) Underwood
Fras. Searson
Thomas ( ) Ashby

Wit: R. Stace [?]
20 Nov. 1734. Ack. and OR.

Pages 16-17. Will of Thomas Simson, dated 13 Oct. 1734.
Thomas Simson of Prince William County, carpenter, being very sick and weak of body.

Unto my oldest son William Simson one hundred and twenty three acres of land where he is now living on both sides of Sande Run.

Unto my son Baxter Simson two hundred acres of land lying on both sides of Sande Run and aioyning to the land aforesaid of my son William Simson on the uper side, one breeding mare, my bullet gun, one bed bolster, one rug and two blankets, one iron pot, six plates and six spoons.

To my son Thomas Simson three hundred and eighty six acres of land lying on the south side of Chapawamsik Creek, likewise one breeding mare, one feather bed, boulster, rug and two blankets, one iron pot, six plates and six spoons.

Unto my loving daghter Mary Woodard one hundred acres of land where she is now seated and lying on the north side of Sande Run.

Unto my daghter Ann Simson after her mother in laws deceas one cow and calf, one feather bed, boulster, rug and two blankets.

Unto my beloved grand children the son and daghter of Mary Woodward, Thomas Woodward and Ann Woodward, one yew a peace.

Unto my ever loving wife Jane Simson all my plantacion and liberty of one hundred acres of land where I now live [during] her life and after her deceas to fall to my son Baxter. I also give her the priviledg of the whole track for timber for the use of the plantation. I also leave my wife all my moveable estate except the legecies herein before mentioned and leave my wife my whole and sole executor of this my last will and testament, and further I leave my three children Baxter Simson and Thomas Simson to be brought up till they come to the age of eighteen years and likewise my daghter Ann till she come of age by my wife Jane Simson. I further leave my daghter Ann to Mary Woodard in case her mother dies before she comes of age.

I further give unto my wife two negroes during her life and after her deceace for to be equally divided among my children.

Wit:
Thos. Ford
John Robertson
Mary (X) Evans

Thomas (T) Simson

1734/35

19 Nov. 1734. Presented into Court by Jane Simson Executrix therein named. Proved by the oaths of Thomas Ford and John Robertson, two of the witnesses.

Page 18. Bond of Jane Simpson, John Ferguson and Job Carter unto Robert Jones, first justice. For ₤200. 19 Feb. 1734. Jane Simpson is extx. of Thomas Simpson, dec.
        Jane (M) Simpson
        John Ferguson
        Job Carter

Wit: Thomas Robinson
19 Feb. 1734. Ack. and OR.

Page 19. Inventory of the estate of John Underwood, dec., made in obedience to order of 20 Nov. 1734. Appraisers sworn before Collo. Thos. Harrison.
 Total valuation ₤ 4.7.0. Richd. Higgins
          Robert Hedges
          Henry Nelson

14 Dec. 1734. Sworn before Thos. Harrison.
19 Feb. 1734. George Underwood returned this inventory and appraisment.

Pages 19-20. Will of Martha Lillard, dated 17 Jan. 1734.
 Martha Lillard of the Parish of Truro in the County of Prince William being sick and weak of body.
 To my sone Marcellus Littlejohn one third part of all my estate to [be] paid him at the age of twenty one years.
 Unto my daughter Mary Littlejohn one third part of all my estate to be paid her at the age of eighteen years or at the day of her marriage.
 To my daughter Sarah Lillard one third part of all my estate to be paid her at the age of eighteen years or at the day of her marriage.
 And if it should so happen that either of my children should die before they arrive to the age as aforesaid my will is that his or her part goe to the survivour or survivours of them and if it should so happen that they should all die before they arrive to the ages as aforesaid then to goe to my loving sister Mary Bosman and heirs.
 I do appoint Thomas Bosman to be my executor and to take care of my children untill they shall arrive to the ages as aforesaid.   Martha (M) Lillard
Wit:
John Furguson
John Hargford
Francis Coffer
 20 Feb. 1734. Presented in Court by Thomas Bosman executor therein named. Proved by the oaths of the witnesses.

Pages 20-21. Bond of Thomas Bosman and Jeremiah Bronaugh unto Robert Jones, first justice. For ₤ 50. 20 Feb. 1734. Thomas Bosman is exor. of Martha Lillard, dec.
        Thomas (X) Bosman
        Jere Bronaugh

Wit: Thomas Robinson
20 Feb. 1734. Ack. and OR.

Page 21. Inventory of the estate of John Manley, made pursuant to order of 20 Nov. 1734.
Total valuation £ 60.15.0.
Appraisers set apart that part of the personal estate belonging to John Manley in the hands of Richd. Osborn, Gent., as appeared by the inventory of his Deceased father's estate to be his due. 22 Nov. 1734. Tho. Lewis
John Minor
John Sturman

Sworn before Lee Barker.
20 Feb. 1734. Ret. and OR.

Page 22. Bond of John Madden, John Harl and Ralph Hughes unto Robert Jones, first justice. For £ 50. 20 Feb. 1734. John Madden is admr. of Neal Foster, dec.
John Madden
John Harl
Ralph (R H) Hughes

Wit: Thomas Robinson

Page 23. Account of estate of Thomas Kerfoot, dec.
1735 To Credit to Henry Boggess £ 0.3.0
Cr
By David Grant 0.1.6
Tobacco Account
To paid William Harll for you 100
To paid Wm. Davey by your order 50
By Edward Doyle 20
By Mr. William Godfrey 448
9 Jan. 1734.
Edwd. Barry
20 Feb. 1734. Edward Barry exhibited this account.

Pages 23-24. Will of John Fishback, dated 11 March 1735.
John Fishback att Licking run in Prince William County being very sick and weak
Unto my loving wife Meary Doarterty the turd of all my movables and for to have house and land During hir life and after her Decease it shall fall to my son John Fedrick Fishback living on the soute side of Licking Run runing towards the Mass [Maff?]
To my son Henry Fishback on the north side of the said licking run fifty more or less.
To my daughter Catren Recttor fifty eaquers of land more or less whereon Henry Hager doth live. The said land Runs along John Hoffmans line. I give my daughter Elizabeth Fishback a hunders eakers of land more or less living betwixt Millkird Bromback and George Gent.
Unto my son John Frederick Fishback a hunder and tunty eakers of land mor or less liuing on the sout east side of Chandore on Carter Line.
To my sons Harman Fishback, John Jacob Fishback, John Phiplip Fishback and Jessie Fishback ten hunder and tunty aite akers of land for to be divided in four parts every one having a eaquell share of the said land liing on Hunger Runn on the Branch of Goose Creek.

1734/35

    To my sone Henry Fishback two hundred eaker of land more or less in the little fork of Raphnack on the North River.
    I give my son Fredrick Fishback a two year old muar.
    To my sone Henry Fishback a tow [sic] year old muar.
    Unto Jacob Fishback my cousin one cow and a calf at the end of tow [sic] years for his sarvatude.
    I give my wife Meary Doterty one gray horse for the youse of the plantation.
    I do constitute John Kamper and an nomnate and apoint Harmon Fishback my and to be my whole and sole execters.
Wit: Jno Fishback
George Gent
Jacob Holtzclaw
Joseph Martin
John Recteor
    19 March 1734. Presented into Court by John Kamper and Harman Fishback executors therein named. Proved by the oaths of George Gent, Jacob Holtzclaw and Joseph Martin three of the witnesses thereto.

Pages 25-26. Bond of John Kamper, Harman Fishback, Brian Connely, George Gent and Joseph Martin unto Francis Awbrey, Gent., first justice. For £200. 19 March 1734. John Kemper and Harman Fishback are exors. of John Fishback, dec.
                      John Kamper
                      Harman Fishback
                      Bryan (X) Conelly
                      George Gent
                      Joseph Martin
  Wit: Catesby Cocke, Thomas Robinson.
  19 March 1734. Ack. and OR.

Pages 26-27. Bond of Ann Russel, Valentine Barton and Isaac Ferguson unto Francis Awbrey, first justice. For £50. 19 March 1734. Ann Russel is admx. of William Bean, dec.
                      Ann (A) Russel
                      Vall. Barton
                      Isaac Ferguson
  Wit: Thos. Robinson.
  19 March 1734. Ack. and OR.

Pages 27-28. Inventory of the estate of Martha Lillard, dec., made pursuant to order of 20 Feb. 1734.
    No total valuation.
    8 March 1734.   John Farguson
                                John Heryford
                                William Peake
    20 March 1734. Thomas Bosman returned this inventory and appraisment.

Pages 28-29. Will of Michael Ashford, dated 20 Oct. 1734.
    Michael Ashford of Prince William County, Virginia, being sick and weak in body.
    To my son John one horse named Roger and one black foal and two cows and two calves.
    To my son Michael a horse called his and a young bay mare and two cows and two calves.

To my son William a bay horse called his own and two cows and two calves.

To my son Michael all that tract of land lying on the head of Doge Run and 1 feather bed with the furniture.

To my sons George and William that tract of land at Doge Run not before bequeathed to be equally divided between them allowing their brother Michael Timber sufficient to supply his necessity.

To my sone John a tract of land lying between Doge Run and little Hunting Creek and one feather bed with the Blanketts and rugg and sheets belonging to it.

To my daughter Ann a little white horse called credit.

To my son George a black mare which came of a Dun mare.

To my daughters Mary and Constance two filly foals between them.

I do constitute appoint and ordain my loving wife to be my sole executrix.

To my son George one negro named Dick.

Unto my son John that tract of land upon the head of Auatinck.

Unto my son William 1 bed with the rugg blanketts and sheets belonging to it.

Unto my sons George and William one bed a piece with the ruggs blanketts and sheets belonging to them.

Unto my daughter Ann, Mary and Constance each of them one bed and furniture with the ruggs blanketts and sheets belonging to them.

I do constitute and appoint my well beloved wife my sole executrix.
                      Mic. Ashford

Wit:
John Camplin
Joshua (I) Oxely

20 March 1734. Presented into Court by John Ashford. Proved by the oaths of the witnesses thereto subscribed. Ann Ashford sole executrix appointed in the said will being dead without having first undertaken the burthen of the execution thereof, on the motion of the said John Ashford certificate is granted him for obtaining letters of administration with the said will annext.

Page 30. Bond of John Ashford, Thomas Smith and Edward Embs unto Denis McCarty, first justice. For £300. 20 March 1734. John Ashford is admr. with will annexed of Michael Ashford.
                      John Ashford
                      Thos. Smith
                      Edwd. (E) Emns

Wit: Catesby Cocke, Thomas Robinson.

Pages 31-32. Will of Ann Ashford, dated 25 Nov. 1734.

Ann Ashford of Prince William County, Virginia, being sick and weak in body.

Unto my daughter Ann a young negro boy named Sam.

Unto my daughters Mary and Constance a negro man named Peter and the woman servant named Mary for the time she has to serve.

1734/35

All the pewter belonging to the house to be equally divided amongst all my children as well sons as daughters.
All my hoggs belonging to me to be equally divided amongst all my children.
All my sheep belonging to me to be equally divided amongst all my children.
To my daughter Mary a horse named Champion.
To my daughter Constance a horse named Shaver.
All the remainder of my cattle not before bequeathed by my husband to be equally divided amongst all my children.
Unto my sone John one ovall table.
To my sone Michael a square table of oak.
A piese of Holland to be equally divided amongst my daughters.
I do constitute ordain and appoint my sone John my sole executor.
All the tobacco that remains clear to the estate when all the debts are paid due from the estate to be equally divided amongst all my children.

Wit: Ann (A) Ashford
John Champlin
Joshua (I) Oxley

20 March 1734. Presented in Court by John Ashford executor therein named. Proved by the oaths of the witnesses.

Pages 32-33. Bond of John Ashford, Thomas Smith and Edward Emns unto Dennis McCarty, the first justice. For £ 300. 20 March 1734. John Ashford is exor. of Ann Ashford.

                    John Ashford
                    Thos. Smith
                    Edward (E) Emns

Wit: Catesby Cocke, Thomas Robinson.
20 March 1734. Ack. and OR.

Pages 33-34. Inventory and appraisement of the third part of the estate of Capt. Charles Broadwater set aside for Mrs. Eliza. Broadwater in obedience to order of 21 Aug. 1734.
Includes 8 negroes valued at £ 76.
Total valuation £ 116.4.7.
                    Thos. Lewis
                    Thos. Smith

20 March 1734. Ret. and OR.

Page 35. Will of Jacob Gibson, dated 2 Oct. 1734.
Prince Will County
Jacub Gibson of above sd. County.
To my son Jacob Gibson my gray hors that I had of Margarit Russell.
To my son Abraham Gibson one young gray horse coled Darrick and my bridell and sadell.
To my daughter Mary Parker one young hofer.
To my daughter Sarah Lambath one yarling.
To my daughter Jann Turner one young mair.
To my son Iasack Gibson one young cow.
To my daughter Ann Gibson one young cow.

All the remainder part of my astate to my loving wife Jane Gibson, land and livungs to be disposd after hur one discration and firder I do apint my wife to be my hole and sol axitor and I do desier my astate should not be brout to apraisment but that it may be divided according to my will by some of the nighburs.
Wit: Jacub (X) Gibson
Leo Barker
George Calvard Junr.
   21 May 1735. Presented into Court by Jane Gibson wido. executrix therein named. Proved by the oaths of the witnesses.

Pages 35-36. Bond of Jane Gibson, Leonard Barker and Valentine Barton unto Denis McCarty, Gent., first justice. For £40. 21 May 1735. Jane Gibson is extx. of Jacob Gibson, dec.
                                          Jane (I) Gibson
                                          Leo Barker
                                          Val Barton
Wit: Catesby Cooke.
21 May 1735. Ack. and OR.

Pages 36-38. Will of Mark Hardin, dated 16 March 1734.
   Mark Hardin of Princ Wm. County in the Colony of Virginia.
   To my eldest son John Hardin two hundred and thirty two acres of land situate lying and being in Princ William County the said land being part of a paten for six hundred and forty two acors [?] of land and begining for the two hundred and thirty two acres of land at a white oack standing in the first line mentioned in the said paten on the southeast side of the said track of land then runing north west westerly along a sarvanor [?] cawled by the name of Martins Spring branch to a corner hickory standing in the hid [?] of the said Sarvanor, then more westaly to a corner white oack then south west to an whit oack then nothe westerly to a corner five white oacks then nothe esterly to a corner hickory and five white oacks then down the main branch of muddy Hole extending down the said branch to wt oack standing in the said branch blow the house where the said John Hardin at present lives then notherly up a valey to a corner stake being the extent of the said track of land then esterly to a post and so to the white oack where it first begun.
   Unto my son Martin Hardin two hundred and ten acres of land situate lying and being in the said County of Princ Wm. aforesaid, the same being part of the aforesaid track or paten and begining at the abovesaid Hickery and five white oacks then running notherly to the extent of the said track and including all the southwesterly parts of the track.
   Unto my sone Mark Hardin two hundred aceres of land it being the remainer part of the said track as above said in the County of Princ William and allso one negro man cawled Sambo.
   To my sone Henry Hardin two hundred acres of land situate lying and being in Prince William County, the said land being part of three hundred acres of land bought of James McDoneill the said land lying and being on the south side of Kittle Run the loer part of it and the plantation to him.

If any of my three sons last named Martin, Mark or Henry Hardin should die without heirs lawfully begotten that there land shall [go] to two of my daughters Ann and Alis Hardin.

Unto my daughter Elizabeth Hardin one hundred acres of land it being the upper part of three hundred acres of land bought of James McDoniell on the south side of Kittle Run in the County of Prince William.

My will is that all my sons and my daughter Martha (to wit) John, Martin, Mark and Henry Hardin and Martha McDonhill shall have two shillings star[ling] payd to each of them out of my estate and that to be their full part besides there land allready given to my sons and no more.

It is my will that after my decees my loving wife Mary Hardin shall choose her devedent of the land above given to sone Mark Hardin and to be therewith satisfied for her third part of all my lands, that then she shall have the said land and Negro Sambo and all the improvements during her life and after deceas the said land and Negro Sambo and all the improvements to fall to my sone Mark Hardin.

It is my will that after the deceas my whole parsonall estate shall not be brought to appraisment but to be at the deuction of my loving wife Mary Hardin.

It is my will that after my deces of my loving wife Mary Hardin that the above mentioned parsinall estate shall be equally divided amung my five daughters vis. Abgail, Mary, Ann, Elizabeth, Alis or their heirs.

My will is that my loving wife Mary Hardin and son John Hardin and my son Mardin Hardin be my executors.

Wit: Mark Hardin
Thomas (X) Simon
Daniell (X) Shumate
Judith (I) Shumate
Elizabeth (E) Roylte

21 May 1735. Presented into Court by Mary Hardin and John Hardin executors therein named. Proved by the oaths of Thomas Simon and Danl. Shumate, two of the witnesses.

Page 39. Bond of Mary Hardin, John Hardin, Robert Jones and Thomas Conway unto Denis McCarty, first justice. For £ 300. 21 May 1735. Mary Hardin and John Hardin are exors. of Mark Hardin, dec.
                                             Mary (X) Hardin
                                             John Hardin
                                             Robt. Jones
                                             Thomas Conway

Wit: G. Turbervile
21 May 1735. Ack. and OR.

Page 40. Inventory of the estate of William Bean made pursuant to order of 19 March 1734.
Total valuation £ 5.19.5.
Ann (A) Rusell, administrator
                                             Antho. Seale
                                             John (I) Young
                                             Jacob (I) Smith

21 May 1735. Ann Russell administratrix of William Bean, dec., returned this inventory and appraisment.

Page 40. Bond of Ann Mason, John Mercer, John Gregg, James Baxter and Catesby Cocke unto the Worshipfull Justices of Prince William County. For ₤ 5000. 21 May 1735. Ann Mason and John Mercer are guardians of George, Mary and Thomson Mason, orphans.
        Ann Mason
        J. Mercer
        John Gregg
        James Baxter
        Catesby Cocke
 Wit: Thomas Robinson
 21 May 1735. Ack. and OR.

Page 41. Bond of William Shadburn and Richard Blackburn, Gent., unto the Worshipfull Justices of Prince William County. For ₤ 20. 21 May 1735. William Shadburn is guardian of Mary and Jane Shadburn, orphans.
        William Shadburn
        R. Blacburn
 Wit: Thomas Robinson
 21 May 1735. Ack. and OR.

Pages 41-42. Bond of William Harle and Lewis Elzey unto Denis McCarty, first justice. For ₤ 20. William Harle is admr. of John Rhodry, dec.
        William (H) Harle
        Lewis Elzey
 Wit: Thomas Robinson
 21 May 1735. Ack. and OR.

Page 42. Account of estate of William Bean.
 Ann (A) Russell signed the account.
 21 May 1735. Ann Russell admx. of the estate of William Bean, dec., presented this account in Court.

Pages 42-43. Inventory and appraisment of estate of John Fishback.
 Total valuation ₤ 56.13.7.
 5 May 1735.
        Jno. Wright
        Jacob Holtzclaw
        Jeffery Johnson
 Hermanus Fishback signed the inventory.
 21 May 1735. Herman Fishback executor of John Fishback, dec., returned this inventory and appraisment.

Page 44. Bond of William Shadborn and Edward Feagan unto Denis McCarty, first justice. For ₤ 20. 21 May 1735. William Shadborn is admr. of John Shadborn, dec.
        William Shadborn
        Edward (E) Feagin
 Wit: Thos. Robinson
 Ack. and OR 21 May 1735.

Page 45. Bond of John Ashford, Thomas Smith and Edward Emms unto Dennis McCarty, Gent., justice. For ₤ 300. 23 May 1735. John Ashford is admr. with will annexed of Michael Ashford, dec.
        John Ashford
        Thos. Smith
 Wit: James Baxter Edward (E) Emms
 23 May 1735. Ack. and OR.

1735

Page 46. Inventory of Neal Foster's estate.
   Total valuation ₤ 8.19.3.
   John Madden signed the inventory.
                              John (T) Homs
                              Edward (E) Feagins
                              William (X) Fluher
   22 May 1735. John Madden returned this inventory and appraisment.

Pages 46-47. Will of William Sparkes, dated 24 Nov. 1734.
   William Sparkes of Prince William County, Virginia, being sick and weak in body.
   I do constitute ordain and appoint my well beloved wife my sole executrix of all my stock of cattell, hoggs, household stuff or any thing or things whatsoever now belonging to me the same to dispose and make use of as she thinks proper and no other person or persons whatsoever. And after my wife's decease my desire is that James Brown or William Gadds [?] do possess the same.
Wit: William (W) Sparks
John Champlin
Bridget (X) Knowland
   18 June 1735. Presented in Court by Mary Sparks sole executrix. Proved by the oaths of the witnesses.

Page 47. Bond of Mary Sparks and Thomas Smith unto Denis McCarty, first justice. For ₤ 100. 18 June 1735. Mary Sparks is extx. of William Sparks.
                              Mary (X) Sparks
                              Thos. Smith
   Wit: Catesby Cocke
   18 June 1735. Ack. and OR.

Pages 48-49. Estate of Phillip Nowland.

	[tobo.]	[₤]
To Edward Barry by Judgement	997	
To Ann Middleton per Acct prov'd for 7 bbl. of corn at 10/ per and 300 lb. Tobacco	420	3.10. 0
To Henry Bogss per acct. proved		0. 6. 0
To William Godfrey for parish levies	399	
To Timothy McCan per acct. proved	220	
To Derby Bryand by acct. proved	230	
To Michael Regan per judgment	169	
To Saml. Smith per Rect.		0.13. 6
To John Musgrove per accounts proved	230	1. 5. 0
To John Carrol per acct. proved 2 bbs. Corn		1. 0. 0
To Thos. Clayborn Gent. for Clks fees	124	
To John Quin per Judgmt.	932	0. 5. 0
To Levies Clerks and Sherifs fees pd. Thos. Hawley	856	
To Pierce Noland per Acct. proved	2144	6.16. 6
To Thos. Edge per acct. proved for wages	500	
To Mr. Catesby Cocke per Acct.		7.17. 7
To Coll. Mason for rent	1000	
To Bryan Conner for freedom dues		3.10. 0
To Mr. George Noble per Rect.	546	

```
      To Derby Bryant per Acct. proved            340
      To Stephen Lewis per Acct. proved                    1.19. 5
      To Capn. John Colvin                       1200
      To Clks Sheriffs and Lawyers fees in the
         suite of Henry Bryan agt. the Decd. etc. 273
      To Eliz. Carrol for her portion left per
         her father                              1264
      To Luke Carrol for his portion left per
         his father                              1264
      To Danel Carol per Judgmt pd. to Mr. Mercer 816
      To Daniel French per the Deced. Note of
         Hand                                     425
      To Capn. Awbrey paid him                    130
      To Edward Broughton for settling the accts. 150
      To Clk. Sureta and Sheriffs fees paid
         Saml. Smith                              456
                                   Bridget (X) Noland
      18 June 1735. Bridget Noland presented in Court this account.
```

Pages 49-50. Inventory of estate of George Mason made in obedience to order of 21 May 1735.
    Includes 7 negroes valued at £ 102.
    One mulatto woman named Ann Wilson   19. 0. 0
    One servant man named John Webb   5. 0. 0
    One servant Do named Morgan Carpenter   7. 0. 0
    Total valuation £ 304.19.7 3/4.
                        John Farguson
                        John Hereford
                        William Champneys
    18 June 1735. Ret. and OR.

Pages 50-51. Inventory of estate of John Shadburn, dec., made in obedience to order of 21 May 1735.
    Total valuation £ 5.17.4.
    William Shadburn signed the inventory.
                        Benja. Bullett
                        Thos. Ashbee
                        Richd. Wisdell
    18 June 1735. Returned by William Shadburn.

Page 51. The debts which was owing to Richd. Melton Decd. and lately recd. which ware not set down in the inventory and pd. as follows unto Elizabeth Melton his widdow
    By the widdow Davies   180 [lbs. tobo.]
    By Richard Davies   37
    By Robert Bland   70
    Wm. Baily   25
    Mr. John Diskin   40
    17 Sept. 1734.   Elizabeth (E) Higgs
    18 June 1735. Elizabeth Higgs returned this additional inventory and appraisment of the estate of Richard Melton, dec.

Page 51. Inventory of estate of John Rhodry, dec., made pursuant to order of 21 May 1735. Appraisers sworn before Capt. Francis Awbrey.

1735

Total valuation ₺ 3.7.-
Wm. (H) Harl signed the inventory
         Robert Bates
         John Summers
         Gerard Trammel
 18 June 1735. William Harl returned this inventory and appraisment of the estate of John Rhodery, dec.

Page 51. Account of estate of John Rhodry.
 To paid Henry Hamilton as per acct
   proved   55 [lbs. tobo.]
         William (H) Harl
 18 June 1735. William Harl produced this account.

Pages 52-53. Bond of Jane Farrow, Thomas Harrison, Junr., and Stephen Delisle unto Denis McCarty, first justice. For ₺ 200. 18 June 1735. Jane Farrow is admx. of John Farrow, dec.
         Jane (I) Farrow
         Thos. Harrison Junr.
         Stephen Delisle
 Wit: Thos. Robinson
 18 June 1735. Ack. and OR.

Page 53. Bond of John Diskin and Thomas Osborn, Gent., unto the Worshipfull Justices of Prince William County. For ₺ 200. 18 June 1735. John Diskin is guardian of Ruebin Pagett, orphan.
         John Diskin
         Thomas Osborne
 Wit: Thos. Robinson
 18 June 1735. Ack. and OR.

Page 54. Will of William Glegg, dated 4 May 1734.
 To Honor Glegg my loveing wife all my lands, livings, goods and chattles, moveables and immoveables for ever to be at her own disposing and hath liberty to sell or morgage any of the above saide lands, liveings, goods and chattles, she being my hole and sole Axaititore.
Wit: William (W) Glegg
Thomas Jones
Mary (N) Johnson
 18 June 1734. Proved by the oaths of the witnesses.
 In obedience to an order of Court we have administred the oath of an executr. to Honor Glegg late Honor Crandin [sic] and she made oath that this is the last will and testament of William Glegg. 12 July 1735. William Hackney
         John Allen
 16 July 1735. Honour Crandon late Honour Glegg sole executrix having made oath to this will, it is admitted to record.

Pages 54-56. Inventory of estate of William Sparks, made in obedience to order of 18 June 1735.
 Total valuation ₺ 35.6.9
         John Ashford
         John Musgrove
         Michael Ashford
 Mary (X) Sparkes signed the inventory.

A crop of tobacco and other things sold before the
    appraisement   £ 5.10.6
17 July 1735. Returned and adm. to rec.

Pages 56-57. Inventory and appraismt. of Cornelius Jones'
estate.   6 July 1734.
  Total valuation £ 45.12.5.
  Elizabeth (E) Cooper signed the inventory.
                               Valentine Peyton
                               Wm. (M) Davis
                               John Goslin
  Appraisers sworn before Benja. Grayson.
  16 July 1735. Elizabeth Cooper late Elizabeth Jones admx.
of the estate of Cornelius Jones, dec., returned this inventory
and appraisment.

Page 57. Will of John Miliord Fiter, dated 28 Aug. 1735.
  Jno. Miliord fiter of the County of Prince Wm. being sick
and weke of body.
  Unto my sister Mary Fishback a fore year old mare and cow
and calf, too sow shotes.
  Unto my lafull wife Mary all the remaner part of my estate
movebeles or unmovebel, persen or Riel.
  I do constistute nominate and apint my well beloved wife
Mary to be my hole and sole Exetrx.
Wit: Jno. (I) Mileord fiter
George Gent
John Holtzclaw
Wm (X) Biding
  17 Sept. 1735. Presented into Court by Mary Fiter executrix
therein named. Proved by the oaths of the witnesses.

Page 58. Bond of Mary Fiter, George Gent and John Holtzclaw
unto Denis McCarty, Gent., first justice. For £ 50. 17 Sept.
1735. Mary Fiter is extx. of Miliord Fiter, dec.
                               Mary (X) Fiter
                               George Gent
                               John Holtzclaw

  Wit: Thos. Robinson
  17 Sept. 1735. Ack. and OR.

Pages 58-59. Will of Christopher Winsor, dated 30 June 1735.
  Christofor Winsor of Prince William being sick in body.
  To my loving wife Sarah Winsor the third part of my whole
estate both parsanal or reaill.
  To my son Thos. Winsor the plantation I now live on and
half the that said track of land and my gun and a   [sic]
  To my sone William Winser the other half of the same track
of land lying on Auatink and Pohick Run.
  To my son Christifor Winser one hundred acres of land
lying on or near Neaph wack [?] Run.
  After my just debts paid I leave the rest of my whole
estate to be equally divided between my said children Ann,
Thos., William, Mary, Christofor, Sarah and Jane.
  I leave my loving wife whole and soull Exectr. of this my
last will and testament and desire my estate may not be

1735

apraisel but be divided by three such men as my wife shall think fitt.
   I furder desire my children may continue with their mother untill they come to full age of twenty one years.
Wit: Christifor (X) Winsor
Wm. West
James (X) Murrey
   17 Sept. 1735. Presented into Court by Sarah Winser sole executrix. Proved by the oaths of the witnesses.

Pages 59-60. Bond of Sarah Winsor, John Sturman and Samuel Connier unto Denis McCarty, first justice. For ₤ 100.
17 Sept. 1735. Sarah Winsor is extx. of Christopher Winser, dec.
                            Sarah (X) Winser
                            John Sturman
   Wit: Thos. Robinson   Samuel (X) Connier
   17 Sept. 1735. Ack. and OR.

Pages 60-61. Inventory of estate of Mr. John Farrow, dec., made 8 Aug. 1735 in obedience to order of 18 June 1735. Appraisers sworn before Mr. John Diskin.
   Includes 3 negro men valued at ₤ 84.
   Total valuation not given.
                            Burr Harrison
                            Henry Nelson
                            Richd. Higgins
                            Joseph Davis
   17 Sept. 1735. Returned and adm. to rec.

Page 62. Inventory of William Glegg estate made in obedience to order of 16 July 1735. Appraisers sworn before Robert Jones, Gent.
   To one servant Mary Phillips   ₤ 5. 0. 0
   Total valuation ₤ 30.9.9
   11 Aug. 1735.   Samuel Earle
                            Willm. Blackwell
   19 Sept. 1735. Returned.   Joseph Blackwell
   Memdm. There was sold and delivered before the appraisment
To Mr. Joseph Blackwell two cows and calves
To Mr. Jos. Hudnal one cow and yearling
To Capn. Benja. Bereman one cow

Page 63. Inventory of estate of Thomas Simpson, dec.
   Includes 2 negro men, 1 man servant, 1 woman servant.
   Not appraised.
   15 Oct. 1735.
   Jane (X) Farguson signed the inventory.
   19 Nov. 1735. Returned by Jane Ferguson late Jane Simpson Executx. of Thomas Simpson, dec.

Pages 63-64. Bond of James Thatcher, Stephen Lewis and Cavan Dulany unto Denis McCarty, justice. For ₤ 50. 19 Nov. 1735. To indemnify Mary Thatcher as admx. of Thomas Albin, dec.
                            James Thatcher
                            Cav Dulany
   19 Nov. 1735. Ack. and OR.   Stepn. Lewis

Pages 64-65. Will of Thomas Furr, dated 3 Nov. 1734.
Thomas Furr of Hamilton Parish in the County of Prince William being sick of body.
Unto Malachi Cummings one hundred acres of land whereon he now lives during his life and his wifes life the said Malachi Cummings to make no waste nor sale of timber only for the plantatein etc. and after the decease of them and my wife the said two hundred acres of land to fall to her son Thos.
Unto my loving wife Elizabeth Furr all my household goods cattle, horses, mares, hoggs, sheep that in any wise belongs to me.
After my wife Elizabeth's decease that plantation whereon her son Thos. lives to her heirs and in case of his death to fall to her son William.
After my wife's decease the plantation whereon I now live to her son William and after the decease of my loving wife what household stuff, goods and stock there is to be eaqually divided between her two sons Thos. and William except one pewter dish which I leave unto her daughter Elizabeth Cummings.
I desire Jonathan Gibson when he lays of his land to lay of mine with it and for what land William Allen has taken from me to get it again if possible and let the children have a part as otherwise if he does not like of it take it out of the estate.
I desire that if John Lattimore is disturbed about his land and will lay it off to have it done by a sworn surveyor and chain carryers and if any be wanting to take it where he knoct off.
Unto my loving wife one servant woman and an orphan boy called by the name of Thos. Mcantier.
It is my will that my wife have all my tobacco, debts due and whatsoever belongs to me.
I do make, ordain and constitute my loving wife my executrix of this my last will and testament to see it performed and furthermore I do ordain and appoint my loving friend Jonathan Gibson overseer and assistant to my wife.

Wit: Thoms. (X) Furr
John Boystone
Ralph (R H) Hues
Thos. (T) Cummings
19 Nov. 1735. Presented in Court by Elizabeth Furr Executrix. Proved by the oaths of the witnesses.

Pages 65-66. Inventory of estate of Christopher Winsor, dec.
Not appraised.
Sarah Winser, executrix, signed the inventory.
19 Nov. 1735. Sarah Winsor, executrix, presented this inventory which was OR.

Page 66. Account of the estate of Christopher Winsor.
Sarah Winsor, extx., signed the account.
19 Nov. 1735. Sarah Winser exhibited this account which was OR.

Pages 66-67. Bond of John Brown, Hugh West, Lewis Elzey and Thomas Smith unto Francis Awbrey, Gent., first justice. For

1735/36

₤ 50. 17 March 1735. John Brown and Hugh West are admrs.
of John Frost, dec.
       John Brown
       Hugh West
       Lewis Elzey
       Tho: Smith

 Wit: Willm. Baker
 17 March 1735. Ack. and OR.

Pages 68-69. Bond of Richard Rutter, John Gladden and Gerrard Trammill unto Francis Aubrey, Gent., justice. For ₤ 50. 17 March 1735. Richard Rutter is admr. of George Goodin, dec.
       Richard Rutter
       John Gladin
 Wit: Willm. Baker Gerrard (I T) Tramml
 17 March 1735. Ack. and OR.

Pages 69-70. Bond of Solomon Organ, Thomas Smith and Gerrard Trammill unto Francis Aubrey, Gent., justice. For ₤ 50. 17 March 1735. Solomon Organ is admr. of Matthew Organ, dec.
       Solomon Organ
       Thoms. Smith
 Wit: Willm. Baker Gerrard (I T) Trammll
 17 March 1735. Ack. and OR.

Page 70. Bond of Thomas Whitford, William Hall and Jno. Gladdin unto Francis Aubrey, Gent., justice. For ₤ 50. 17 March 1735. Thomas Whitford is admr. of William Brooshaw, dec.
       Thomas Whitford
       William (X) Hall
 Wit: Willm. Baker John Gladin
 17 March 1735. Ack. and OR.

Page 71. Bond of James Baxter, Lewis Elzey and Valentine Peyton unto the Worspl. Justices of Prince William County. For ₤ 50. 17 March 1735. James Baxter is guardian of Giles Tillett, orphan.
       James Baxter
       Lewis Elzey
       Val Peyton

 17 March 1735. Ack. and OR.

Page 71. Bond of James Muse and John Gregg unto Worspl. Justices of Prince William County. ₤ 150. 20 March 1735. James Muse is guardian of Thomas Arrington, orphan.
       James Mues
       John Gregg
 Wit: Jno. Sturman, Catesby Cocke.
 20 March 1735. Ack. and OR.

Page 72. Inventory of the estate of Willm. Brooshaw, appraised 19 April 1736.
 Total valuation ₤ 10.18.6
       Gabriel Adams
       Robert Bates
       John Summers

 21 April 1736. Thomas Whitford presented this inventory which was OR.

Pages 72-74. Appraisal of estate of William Linton, Gen[t]., presented to appraisers' view by Benjamin Grayson.
    Includes 13 negroes valued at ₤ 230.
    No total valuation given.   Will Dent
                                          James Baxter
                                          Wm. Champneys
                                          William Davis
  William Dent, Jas. Baxter and William Davis sworn before Thomas Osborne.
    William Champneys sworn before Val Peyton.
    21 April 1736. Benj. Grayson presented this inventory which was OR.

Pages 74-75. Appraisal of estate of John Frost, dec., made pursuant to order of 7 March 1735.
    Total valuation ₤ 2.19.0.   Sampson Darrell
                                          John Dunkan
                                          John Ashford
    21 April 1736. OR.

Pages 75-76. Inventory of estate of Mr. Matthew Orgin, dec., made in obedience to order of 17 March 1735. Appraisers first sworn before Mr. Osborn, justice.
    Total valuation ₤ 17.2.9.   Robert Betes
                                        John Summers
                                        John Evans
  Errors excepted by Solomon Orgain.
    21 April 1736. Solomon Organ returned this inventory which was OR.

Page 76. Inventory of estate of George Goodwin. Appraisers sworn before Mr. Osborn, justice.
    Total valuation ₤ 5.11.4   Robert Bates
                                        John Summers
                                        John Evans
  Richard Rutter signed the inventory.
    21 April 1736. Richd. Rutter presented this inventory which was OR.

Page 77. Belonging to the Estate of Giles Tillett not before Inventoryed.
    Anne (A) Champneys signed the inventory.
    21 April 1736. Ann Champneys presented this additional inventory which was OR.

Page 77. A supplementall inventory of the estate of John Tillett, dec.
    Total valuation ₤ 14.13.0.   Richard Simpson
                                        Thos. Hord
                                        William Simpson
  John Turley, Morris Veale, executors.
    21 April 1736. John Turley returned this inventory which was OR.

Pages 78-79. Bond of Samuel King and William Bolling unto Denis McCarty, Gent., justice. For ₤ 50. 21 April 1736.

1736

Samuel King is admr. of William Addison, dec.
                Samll. King
                William (X) Bolling
  Wit: Willm. Baker
  21 April 1736. Ack. and OR.

Pages 79-80. Bond of William Bolling and Samuel King unto Denis McCarty, Gent., justice. For £ 50. 21 April 1736. William Bolling is admr. of George Bolling, dec.
                Willm. (X) Bolling
                Samll. King
  Wit: Catesby Cocke
  21 April 1736. Ack. and OR.

Pages 80-81. Bond of Richard Crupper, Leonard Barker and Benjamin Grayson unto Denis McCarty, Gent., justice. For £ 200. 22 April 1736. Richard Crupper is admr. of William Harthing.
                Richard (R) Crupper
                Leo. Barker
                Benja. Grayson
  22 April 1736. Ack. and OR.

Pages 81-83. Inventory and appraisal of estate of Daniel French, made in obedience to order of 21 April 1736. Appraisers sworn before Wm. Payn, Gent.
    Includes 11 negroes valued at £ 215.
    Total valuation £ 335.15.7, plus corn at £ 8.15.0.
                Geo. Harrison
                Jno. Summers
                Rob. Bates
19 May 1736. Hugh French Excr. of Daniel French, dec., presented this inventory and appraisement which was OR.

Pages 83-84. Bond of Mary Smith, Thomas Jackman and Geoffrey Johnson unto Denis McCarty, Gent., justice. For £ 15. 19 May 1736. Mary Smith is admx. of William Smith, dec.
                Mary (X) Smith
                Thos. Jackman
  Wit: Catesby Cocke   Joeffry Johnson
  19 May 1736. Ack. and OR.

Page 85. The Remainder of the Estate of William Brookshaw, dec.
    To one mare and year old colt   £ 1. 8. -
                Gabriel Adams
                Robbart Bats
  13 May 1736   John Summers
  19 May 1736. Thomas Whitford returned this supplementary inventory of Brookshaw Est. which was OR.

Pages 85-86. The Estate of William Markham, dec. Account.

	[£]	[tobo.]
To William Bruces [?] Judgmt	0. 2. 7	129
To Mr. Hugh French per Account proved		125
To Thos. Mountjoy per Debt proved	2. 3. 0	
To William Addams per Acct provd.	1. 6. 0	
To James Mousley per Acct provd.		160
To William Rout per Do provd.	0. 5. 0	

To John Shillon [Shelton?] per Do provd.   1. 3. 6
To John Harden per Judgment   2. 6. 7½   120
To Joseph Waugh per Acct proved   313
To Joseph Bohannan per Do   1. 4. -
To James Suddath per Do   99
To William Blackwell per Do   4. 6
To Timothy Dargan per Do   2. 4. 1
To John Catlet per Accout. provd. and
    Judgmt   163
To John Shoemake Junr. per Judgm.   0.17. 9
To John Bradford pt.   1100
To Thomas Furr per Judgment   94
To paid Mr. William Hackney   3. 7. 7 3/4
To Edward Turner   110
To paid Mosely Battaley Gent.   150
To Mary Carney per acct. proved   224½
To Nathaniel Chapman per Accot. proved   351

By reced. per Jno. Hox   4. 3. 3
By reced. per William Dent   414
By Do   John Bush   0. 6. 6
By Do   Thomas Hudnall   0. 1. 6
By Do   John Taylor   0. 5. 8
Ballance in favor or me   ₤ 2.11. 3
Errors excepted per Thos. Conway.
19 May 1736. Thomas Conway exhibited this account which was OR.

Pages 86-88. The Estate of Mr. Charles Broadwater, dec., to Hugh West. Account.   [tobo.] [₤]
    To paid Mr. Thomas Jennings   3300
    To Do Thomas Bush per Judgment   301
    To Do The Reverd. Mr. Frasur for Funeral
        Sermon   500
    To Do Capt. Colvill per Bill passed to
        Docr. Gibb   600
    To Conyers Judgment paid Mr. Mercer   830
    To paid Mr. Edward Embs psh. Levies   880
    To Abraham Lays share of the crop   944
    To paid Mr. Battaley per Bill   500
    To paid Mr. Baxter for county Levys   220
    To Do Massey per accot. proved   298
    To paid Doctor Coleman per Accot. proved   2. 3. 6
    To paid Thomas Bennett per Accot. proved   339
    To psh. Levy pd. Edward Embs   67
    To paid Edwd. Emms after distress made   87
    To pd. Guy Broadwater part of his Legacy   33.13. 3
    To pd. his widow for her thirds   116. 6. 7
    To pd. Mr. Robt. Jones   428
    To Do Mr. Alexander Scott per Judgment   208
    To Do Mr. William Scutt per Do   100
    To Do Nichos. Grimes for rolling Tobacco   1.10. 0
    To Do for Tanning leather   10. -
    To Do James Ball for Smiths work   80
    To pd. Widow Brabin per Accot proved   15. -
    To quit rents pd. Capt. Awbrey as per receipt   4. 5. -

1736

```
    To pd. Thomas Robinson Judgment              295
    To Do David Thomas per Do                    447
    To pd. Draper for rolling Tobacco            [blank]
    To pd. Mr. Sturman for some services done
      in the estate                                         10. -
    To schooling and accomodations for Charles
      Broadwater in the year 1735 and 1736                  12.10. -
    To pd. Mr. Dulany                                       15. -
    To Do Wm. Payne per Accot. proved            12
    To Do Mr. Richard Osborn per Do              120
    To Do Thomas Glover                                      2. 9
    To Do Mr. Battaley                                      10. 7½
    To Edwd. Heagan per Judgment                 199
    To Thomas Bush per do                        2016
    To pd. Mr. Cocke for Guy Broadwater          1076
    To Do Mr. Dent per Accot. proved                         3. -
    To Elizab. Broadwaters note on me            466
    To Abraham Lay per Accot. proved             110
    To John Summers for building a Tobo. house   500
```

16 June 1736. Then settled and adjusted this account
                              Richd. Osborn
                              James Baxter

   17 June 1736. Hugh West, admr. &c of Charles Broadwater, dec., presented this settlement of the said Decedents estate which was OR.

Pages 88-89. An inventory of all and singular the estate of George Eskridge, Gent., dec.
   Includes 6 negroes valued at £ 129.
   No total valuation.
   Made 27 May 1736 in obedience to order of 19 May 1736. Appraisers sworn before Wm. Payne, Gent.
                            Richd. Osborn
                            John Meryford
                            Thos. Lewis

   16 June 1736. OR.

Page 89. Inventory of estate of Wm. Addison, dec., made pursuant to order of 21 April 1736. Appraisers sworn before Richard Osborn, Gent.
   Total valuation £ 2.7.0.
   Saml. King signed the inventory.
                            Thos. Pearson
                            John Strawn
                            Hugh Rigby

   16 June 1736. OR.

Page 90. Inventory and appraisement of estate of George Bolling, dec. Appraisers sworn before Richard Osborn.
   Total valuation £ 3.6.7¼
   Wm. Bolling signed the inventory.
                            Thos. Pearson
                            John Strawn
                            Hugh Rigby

   16 June 1736. OR.

Pages 90-91. Bond of James Strother, Mosely Battaley and John Peyton unto the Worshipll. Justices of Prince William County. For £ 1200. 16 June 1736. James Strother is guardian of Daniel French, orphan.
        James Strother
        M. Battaley
        John Peyton
 Wit: Catesby Cocke, Jno. Bowie
 16 June 1736. Ack. and OR.

Pages 91-92. Bond of Jane Allen and William Hackney unto Denis McCarty, justice. For £ 40. 16 June 1736. Jane Allen is admx. of George Allen, dec.
        Jane (X) Allen
        Wm. Hackny
 Wit: Jno. Bowie
 16 June 1736. Ack. and OR.

Pages 92-93. Inventory and appraisement of estate of George Allen made at his house.
 Total valuation £ 7.17.3.
        Jno. Boystone
        William Hackney Jun.
        James (X) Harrell
21 July 1736. Jane Allen returned this inventory which was OR.

Page 93. Appraisement of estate of William Smith, dec., made in obedience to order of 19 May 1736. Appraisers sworn before William Hackney, Gent.
 Total valuation £ 2.15.10
        John Blowers
        William Linch
        John Right
21 July 1736. Mary Smith returned this inventory which was OR.

Page 94. Account of estate of William Smith, dec.
 Errors excepted per Mary Smith, adminx.
 21 July 1736. Mary Smith, Adminx. &c of William Smith, dec., exhibited this account which was allowed and OR.

Pages 94-95. Bond of Jane Wallis, Richard Crupper and George Burn unto Denis McCarty, Gent., justice. For £ 20. 18 Aug. 1736. Jane Wallis is admx. of Burr Wallis.
        Jane (I) Wallis
        Richard (R) Crupper
        George Byrn
 18 Aug. 1736. Ack. and OR.

Pages 95-97. Will of Joseph Chapman, dated 26 March 1733.
 Joseph Chapman of Prince William County being sick and weake of body.
 To my son Joseph Chapman my plantation whereon I live and all the tract thereunto belonging which contains one hundred and fifty acres.
 Unto my son Joseph one tract of land adjoyning to the aforesaid tract containing one hundred and twelve acres.
 To my son John Chapman three hundred acres of land, being

the major part of that tract out of which I have given one hundred and twelve acres to my son Joseph.
    To my loving daughter Mary Chapman one cow and calf the same to be a young cow with her first calf.
    To my loving daughter Sarah Chapman one cow and calf the same to be a young cow with her first calf.
    To my loving daughter Violleta Chapman one cow and calf the same to be a young cow with her first calf.
    To my loving daughter Elizabeth Chapman one dow and calf the same to be a young cow with her first calf.
    To my loving daughter Mary Chapman my large family Bible.
    To my dear and loving wife Sarah Chapman all the remaining part of my estate both real and personal and likewise appoint, constitute and ordain my most dear and well beloved wife Sarah Chapman my whole and sole executrix.
Wit: Joseph (I) Chapman
John Chapman Purnell
Jno. Quin
Mary (M) Ashmore
    20 Oct. 1736. Proved by the oaths of John Chapman Purnell and Mary Ashmore and adm. to rec.

Pages 97-98. Bond of Aaron Drummon, Edward Broughton and William Whitesides unto Denis McCarty, Gent., justice. For £100. 20 Oct. 1736. Aaron Drummond is admr. of Robert Caborn, dec.
                                    Aaron Drummond
                                      Edwd. Broughton
                                      Wm. Whitside
    Wit: John Bowie
    20 Oct. 1736. Ack. and OR.

Page 98. Appraisement of estate of John Shadburn, dec., made 20 Oct. 1736 in obedience to order of 21 May 1735.
    Total valuation £ 2.1.8.
                          Benja. Bullett
                          Thos. Ashbee
                          Richard Wisdell
    22 Oct. 1736. William Shadburne returned this inventory which was OR.

Page 99. An inventory taken of the estate of Burr Wallace, dec.
    Total valuation £ 12.10.1½.
                          William Baylis
                          Richd. Hegins
                          John Johnson
    29 March 1737. Jane Wallis presented this inventory and it was OR.

Page 100. A supplemental inventory of the estate of George Eskridge, Gent., dec., appraised 3 Jan. 1736/37.
    No total valuation.
    28 March 1737. Returned and OR

Pages 100-101. Bond of William Bennet, John Duncan and Samuel Conner unto Denis McCarty, Gent., justice. For £ 50. 28 March 1737. William Bennet is admr. of Elizabeth

Brabin [Bralin?]

                                    Wm. (X) Bennett
                                    John Duncan
                                    Saml. (X) Conner

   Wit: John Bowie
   28 March 1737. Ack. and OR.

Pages 101-02. Bond of Lewis Elzey, Gent., and James Baxter unto Denis McCarty, Gent., justice. For £ 70. 28 March 1737. Lewis Elzey, Gent., is admr. of Richard Pallister, dec.
                                    Lewis Elzey
                                    James Baxter

   Wit: John Bowie
   28 March 1737. Ack. and OR.

Page 103. Bond of Leonard Barker, Valentine Barton and Thomas Smith unto Denis McCarty, Gent., justice. For £ 800. 28 March 1737. Leonard Barker is executor of the last will and testament of John Walker, dec.
                                    Leo Barker
                                    Valentn. Barton
                                    Thos. Smith

   Wit: John Bowie
   28 March 1737. Ack. and OR.

Page 104. An inventory of the estate of Robert Caborn, dec. Total valuation £ 6.3.2 3/4.
   24 Dec. 1736.   Edwd. (E) Heagin
                                  Aaron Fletcher
                                  Willm. (X) Fletcher

   28 March 1737. Aaron Drummond presented this inventory and it was OR.

Pages 104-05. Bond of George Harrison and Hugh West unto the Worshipful Justices of Prince County [sic] For £ 200. 28 March 1737. George Harrison is guardian of Susannah Stark [?], orphan.   Geo. Harrison
                                    Hugh West

   Wit: John Bowie
   28 March 1737. Ack. and OR.

Page 105. Bond of Hugh West and George Harrison unto the Worshipful Justices of Prince William County. For £ 100. 28 March 1737. Hugh West is guardian of Mary Harrison, orphan.   Hugh West
                                    Geo. Harrison

   Wit: John Bowie
   28 March 1737. Ack. and OR.

Page 106. Bond of Sarah Chapman and Valentine Barton and William Champneys unto Denis McCarty, Gent., justice. For £ 200. 20 Oct. 1736. Sarah Chapman is extx. of Joseph Chapman, dec.   Sarah (X) Chapman
                                    Val. Barton
                                    Wm. Champneys

   Wit: John Bowie
   20 Oct. 1736. Ack. and OR.

Page 107-08. Will of John Walker, dated 5 Nov. 1736.
    Jno. Walker of Prince William County being weak in body.
    What estate I am possessed with to sons or heirs of Robt. and James Walker, they being the nearest of kin to me, after my debts and legacies are paid, being all born in the Parish of Moreton in Caron Hill in the County of Neathsdale in North Britain.
    To the poor of that parish twenty pounds sterling for ever to be lodge in the hands of the minister or elders of the church to be laid out in lands or what they think proper that the interest of it may support the poor of the parish of Moreton and that there may be a stone erected within the church and engraved thereon capital letters mentioning the donor John Walker Mercht. of Virginia.
    To Mary Stevenson twenty pounds or four thousd. pounds of tobo. at the discretion of my executor.
    I do set at liberty Jno. Campell he not demanding freedom dues, thirty or forty shillings of small goods out of my store to be delivered by my Exor.
    Unto Leonard Barker five yds. of ph_ins [?] thats in my store and things necessary thats in my store to make him a suit of cloaths.
    I do appoint my trusty and well beloved friend Mr. Leonard Barker my whole and sole Exorr.
    Also my lease I bequeath to Barker as I had of Sct. Hancock.
Wit: John Walker
Jno. Bryan
Thomas Bush
George Calvert
    I allow my friend Leonard Barker fifteen per cent for his trouble for receiving and collecting my debts.
Wit: John Walker
Jno. Bryan
Thomas Bush
George Calvert
    28 March 1737. Presented in Court by Leonard Barker the Exor. herein named. Proved by oaths of the witnesses.

Page 108. Will of Henry Hager, dated 10 April 1733.
    Henry Hager, minister of the Word of God among the Germans at Licking Run in Prince Wm. County, being very sick and weak.
    Unto my loving wife Anna Catharina all my estate, goods and chattels whatsoever to her during her Natural life.
    Unto my granddaughter Anna Catharina Fishback one cow and calf.
    After the decease of my wife Anna Catharina I will and ordain that all my estate, goods and chattels whatsoever be then divided amongst my seven grand children Anna Catharina Fishback, John Frederick Fishback, Elizabeth Fishback, and Henry Fishback, Agnes Hoffman, Anna Catharina Hoffman and John Hoffman.
    I do hereby revoke and make void all other and former wills and testaments by me heretofore made.
Wit: H. Hager Verbi Dei Minister
Jacob Holtsclaw
Johan Jost. Minster
Johannes Camper

28 March 1737. Proved by oaths of Jacob Holtzclaw and John Joseph Martin two of the witnesses hereto. There being no executor herein named on the motion of John Hoffman and his giving security certificate was granted him for obtaining letters of administration with the will annexed.

Pages 108-09. Bond of John Hoffman and Jacob Holtsclaw unto Denis McCarty, justice. For £ 100. 28 March 1737. John Hoffman is admr. with the will annexed of Henry Hager, dec.

         Johan Hoffman
         Jacob Holtsclaw

Wit: John Bowie
28 March 1737. Ack. and OR.

Pages 109-10. Bond of Richard Osborn and William Payne, Gent., unto Dennis McCarty, Gent., justice. For £ 50. 28 March 1737. Richard Osborn is admr. of John Camplin, dec.

         Richard Osborn
         Wm. Payne

Wit: John Bowie
28 March 1737. Ack. and OR.

Pages 110-11. Bond of Catesby Cocke and John Gregg unto Denis McCarty, Gent., justice. For £ 50. 29 March 1737. Catesby Cock is admr. of Robert Becket, dec.

         Catesby Cocke
         John Gregg

Wit: Jno. Bowie
29 March 1737. Ack. and OR.

Pages 112-13. The estate of Col. George Mason, dec.

	[tobo.]	[£]
To pd. Mr. Battaley Hoels [?] Judgment v. Saml. Short	2492	
To pd. Capt. Hedgman for Mr. Jones for so much recd. by Jno. Chambers for whom Col. Mason was bound to said Jones	1120	
To Mr. Barradel Clks. and Sher. fees on Account Hoel [?]	180	
To Capt. Hedgman for Jno. Buchanan Accot. agt. Colo. Mason	216	0.17. 6
To Mrs. Eliza. Cooke for her accot. agt. Colo. Mason		2.14. 3
To Mr. Battaley for 2 Attors. fees		1.10. 0
To Fees ads. Grigsby Stafford		0.15. -
To Wm. Cave for his account agst. Colo. Mason		2. 5. 4
To pd. Mr. Deat [?] for Mr. Chrysties accot. agst. Colo. Mason	1400	
To Mr. Jno. Graham for his Accot. proved	502	13.13. -
To pd. Thos. Lewis Chapmans Clks. fees wch. C. Mason was to pay	25	
To Benj. Cave for Clerks fees	27	
To Hugh French for Do	90	
To Thoms. West his Accot. agst. Colo. Mason proved		1.13. 6
To Richard Blackburn for Do		0.18. -
To fees Thompson on Petn.		0.10. -

1737

To Nat. Claiborn Clks. fees	222	
To Colo. Willis for Do	121½	
To pd. Mr. Mercer by Mr. Brown	4475	
To Mr. Cole by Do	1582	
To Mr. Barry by Do	5310	
To Mr. Cole by Do	3406	
To Jno. Keene by Do	224	
To Mr. Cocke	1202	
To Edwd. Hughes	453	
To James Leatherland		0. 5. 0
To Mattw. Moss		2. 0. -
To Wm. Davy		0. 8. 0
To Mr. Brooke		17.13. 3
To Do		29. 0. 0
To Do		2. 3. 4
To Jos. Reid	180	
To Mr. Wm. Dent	210	
To Abram St. Clair	600	
To Mr. Speak by Mr. Dent		8. 9. 4
To Mr. Eilbeck	1195	1.13. 3
To William Williams	2000	
To Nathan Thomas		0. 6. 0
To Mr. Hobsons expences		0. 2. 6
To Mr. Cocke		8. -
To pd. Mr. Carter Quit Rents		42. 1. 3
To Capt. Douglas		1.16. 3
By Mr. Mercers Debt to Colo. Mason	681	6.6 3/4
By Recd. Wm. Whitesides	474	
Ben Drummond	530	
Aaron Fletcher	530	
Mr. Bronaugh for Osborn's note on him	433	
Thomas Gascoigne	1000	
Mr. Jno. Coles	460	
Wm. Matthews Junr.	500	
Ann Morris	583	
Mr. Bronaugh	4473	
Foster Conliff & Compa.	99	
Edwd. Barradell		12.11. 6
Capt. Speere [Spoore?]		17.16. 8
Do		5. 0. -
Mr. Adderton		42.18.10¼
By Capt. Gale		23. 8. -
Mr. Dent		17.17. 7½
Mr. Bronaugh	10254	
Matt Moss		0.12. 9½
Mr. Cocke	2414	
Thoms. Adburn	1000	
Capt. Douglas		0.18. -
To Mr. Neal		0.15. 8
To Mr. Thomas in Maryland Curr. 65.2.1		64. 8. 6½

Errors excepted per Ann Mason

25 April 1737. Ann Mason Widow Admx. &c of George Mason, dec., produced this Accot. All tobacco herein mentioned be rated at fifteen shilling per cent.

Pages 114-15. Bond of John Champ, John Diskin and John Kinchelo unto Denis McCarty, Gent., justice. For £2000. 25 April 1837. John Champ is admr. of Thomas Osborn, Gent., dec.
        John Champ
        John Diskin
        Jno. (X) Kinchilo

Wit: John Bowie
25 April 1737. Ack. and OR.

Pages 115-16. Will of Daniel Oriar, dated 4 Oct. 1736.
  Daniel Oriar of the County of Prince William and Colony of Virga. being very sick and weak in body.
  To my loving son John Oriar that part of my land lying and being between the North side of Goose Run and the south side of the county road.
  To my loving son Daniel Oriar my plantation whereon I now live with the remainder of my land lying and being between the North side of the county road and the south side of Dorrets.
  To my loving son John Oriar one young cow and calf, one three years old mare, one three gallons iron pott, two pewther basons, each one gallon, three new pewther plates to be delivered when he arrives to the age of twenty one years.
  To my loving son Daniel Oriar one young cow and calf, one three year old mare, one four gallons iron pott, one new pottel bason and new deep pewther dish, three new pewther plates to be delivered when he arrives to the age of twenty one years.
  To my loving wife Easter Oriar all the rest of my estate (not before will'd or named). And further my will and desire is that my two sons John and Daniel Oriars beforenamed have each of them two years schooling and I likewise constitute make and ordain my dearly beloved wife, my father in law William Thorn and my brother John Oriar my only and sole executors.
  My will and desire is that my estate be not appraised.

Wit:
John Metcalfe
Richard Warsdell
John Catlett

                        mark
                        Daniel (Lanson[?]) Orear
                        his

  25 April 1737. Proved by the oaths of the witnesses. On motion of William Thorn, Hester Oriar and John Oriar (Exors herein named) certificate granted them for obtaining a probate.

Pages 116-17. Bond of Hester Oriar, Wm. Thorn, John Oriar, Thomas Harrison and John Catlet unto Denis McCarty, Gent., justice. For £150. 25 April 1737. Hester Oriar, Wm. Thorn and John Oriar are exors. of Daniel Oriar, dec.
        Hester (X) Oriar
        Willm. (W) Thorn
        Jno. (J) Oriar
        Thos. Harrison Junr.
        John Catlet

Wit: John Bowie
25 April 1737. Ack. and OR.

Pages 117-18. Inventory and appraisement of estate of Henri Hager, made 16 May 1737.

1737

        Total valuation ₤ 49.15.3½.
                                John Joseph Marten
                                John Kemper
                                Peter Hit
    23 May 1737. John Rightor presented this inventory and appraisement which was OR.

Page 118. An account of things forgott at the apraisement of the estate of Christefor Winsor.
        Total valuation ₤ 3.0.0.   Thos. Ovsley
                                    Wm. West
    23 May 1737. Samuel Conner presented this additional inventory which was OR.

Page 119. An inventory of all the goods and chattels of Daniel Orear, dec.
                                Ester (S) Orear
                                Willm. (W) Thorn
                                John Oriar
    23 May 1737. William Thorn presented this inventory which was OR.

Pages 119-20. Appraisement of estate of Elizabeth Brabin, dec. Appraisers sworn before William Payne, Gent.
        Total valuation ₤ 12.15.4.
                                John Sturman
                                John Musgrove
                                Thomas Owsley
    William Bennit, administrator.
    23 May 1737. William Bennet presented this inventory and appraisement which was OR.

Page 120. Appraisement of estate of Richard Pallaster, dec., made in obedience to order of 28 March 1737. Appraisers sworn before Lewis Elzey, Gent.
        Total valuation ₤ 9.13.5½.
                                John Minar
                                Pi Matthews
                                John Glading
    23 May 1737. Lewis Elzey, Gent., presented this inventory and appraisement which was OR.

Page 121. Estate of Thos. Gray, dec.   [tobo.]   [₤]
    To Churchwardens of Hamilton Parish
        Judgt. agt. him   171
    To John Mercer for fee for Petitioning
        Admtion. and settling the account of
        the estate   150
    Jeremh. Bronaugh by account proved and
        Judgmt. from Colo. Harrison with costs 82
    From John Heryford for 1119 lb Tobo. at 2d.   9. 6. 6
    24 March 1735. Errors excepted per Geo. Mason.

    To John Heryford for funeral exps. for burying
        him and his wife
    24 May 1737. John Mercer, Gent., exhibited this account which he formerly settled on behalf of George Mason, Gent.,

dec., who was Admr. of Thomas Gray, dec. The said Mercer made oath that this account was settled, approved of by the Court and as he apprehended was recorded but on search among Masons papers and enquiry found it was not recorded and on the motion of the said Mercer it was admitted to record.

Pages 121-22. Inventory of the estate of Joseph Chapman, dec. made November, 1736. Appraisers sworn before Robert Jones, Gent.
    Total valuation £ 55.4.6.
    Sarah (S) Chapman signed the inventory.
                          Henry Nelson
                          Frans. Seursan
                          John Carr
    24 May 1737. Francis Searsan returned this inventory and appraisement which was OR.

Pages 122-23. Inventory of estate of Robert Becket, dec., made according to order of 26 April 1737.
    Total valuation £ 7.7.9.
                          Jeru. Bronaugh
                          Jere. Bronaugh Junr.
                          John Baxter
    25 May 1737. Catesby Cocke returned this inventory and appraisement which was OR.

Pages 123-26. Inventory of estate of John Walker, dec., made at the plantation of Leonard Barker in obedience to order of 25 April 1737. Appraisers sworn before Robert Jones, Gent.
    No total valuation given.
                          John Gregg
                          Stephen Delisle
                          Willm. Farrow
    27 June 1737. Leonard Barker, Exor. &c of John Walker, dec., returned this inventory and appraisement which was OR.

Page 127. The estate of Robert Howard, dec.   [tobo.]   [£]
    To pd. Mr. Catesby Cocke Judgmt.   361
    To pd. Jno. Lewis' Exors. by Do   881
    By reced. of Solomon Organ   420
    By reced. of John Burk   150
    By reced. of Paul Turly   -. 9. -
    Errors excepted by: John (O) Murphy
                                 Elizabeth (X) Murphy
    27 June 1737. Account allowed and OR.

Page 127. Estate of Robert Caborne, dec. Account dated 27 June 1737.
    Errors excepted by Aaron Drummond.
    27 June 1737. Account allowed and OR.

Page 128. Estate of Geo. Bolling.
    Errors excepted by Wm. Bolling, administrator.
    22 Aug. 1737. Account allowed and OR.

1737

Page 128. Bond of John Turly and Edward Barry unto Worspll. Justices of Prince William County. For £ 100. 22 Aug. 1737. John Turley is guardian of Samuel Tillet, orphan of Giles Tillet, dec.
                                  John Turly
                                  Edwd. Barry
   Wit: John Bowie
   22 Aug. 1737. Ack. and OR.

Pages 129-30. Bond of Catesby Cocke and John Bowie unto Denis McCarty, Gent., justice. For £ 20. 22 Aug. 1737. Catesby Cocke is admr. of Benjamin Hutton, dec.
                                  Catesby Cocke
                                  Jno. Bowie
   Wit: John Diskin, Lewis Elzey
   22 Aug. 1737. Ack. and OR.

Pages 130-31. Bond of Mary Ashmore, Joseph Guess and John Carr unto Denis McCarty, Gent., justice. For £ 300. 22 Aug. 1737. Mary Ashmore is admx. of John Ashmore, dec.
                                  Mary (M) Ashmore
                                  Joseph (I) Guess
   Wit: John Bowie   John (I C) Carr
   22 Aug. 1737. Ack. and OR.

Pages 131-33. Inventory and appraisement of estate of Thomas Osbone [sic], dec., made 9 May 1737.
   Includes 11 negroes at £ 163.0.0
   Servant boy named Jno. Cooper   £ 5.10.0
   Total valuation £ 304.3.12.
                                  Sct. Hancock
                                  Thos. Stribling
                                  Stepn. Delisle
   John Champe, adminr.
   22 Aug. 1737. John Champe, Gent., Adminr. &c of Thomas Osborn, Gent., dec., returned this inventory and appraismt. which was OR.

Page 134. Will of James Henderson, dated 4 June 1735.
   James Henderson in the County of Prince William being very sick and weak in body.
   I give my well beloved friend Jeffery Johnson whom I likewise constitute and ordain my only and sole executor of this my last will and testament all and singular my moveables and lands by him freely to be possed and enjoyed.
Wit: James Henderson
John Right
Thos. Jackman
John Bowling
   But after a second thought I considered that my well beloved friend John Bowlin having a great deal of trouble with me in my sickness and for buearing me my will is that he shall have my mare and colt and gun the 7th day of June 1735.
Wit: James Henderson
Thos. Jackman
Jas. (X) Hann
John (X) Walker

26 Sept. 1737. Proved by the oaths of John Wright and Thomas Jackman, two of the witnesses thereto, and the codicil by the oath of Thomas Jackman one of the witnesses. On motion of Jeffry Johnson the Exor. and his performing what is usual in such cases certificate is granted him for obtaining a probate.

Page 135. Bond of Jeffery Johnson, Thomas Jackman and John Right unto Denis McCarty, Gent., justice. For £ 50. 26 Sept. 1737. Jeffrey Johnson is exor. of James Henderson, dec.
        Jeffrey (X) Johnson
        Thos. Jackman
        John Right
Wit: John Bowie
26 Sept. 1737. Ack. and OR.

Pages 136-37. Bond of Catesby Cocke and John Colvill unto Denis McCarty, Gent., justice. For £ 20. 26 Sept. 1737. Catesby Cocke is admr. of John Tarph, dec.
        Catesby Cocke
        John Colvill
Wit: Jno. Bowie.
27 Sept. 1737. Ack. and OR.

Page 137. Inventory of estate of John Camplin, dec., appraised 29 June 1737.
 Total valuation £ 0.8.0.
 Richard Osborn, admr.   Thos. Lewis
        Jos. Cash
        Wm. King
27 Sept. 1737. Richard Osborn, Gent., presented this inventory and appraisement which was OR.

Pages 137-38. Appraisement of estate of Thoms. Albin, dec., made 14 Aug. 1736 according to directions of an order of 25 July 1736.
 Total valuation £ 24.15.3. Richard Wood
        John Grantham
        Amos Sinkelar
27 Sept. 1737. Mary Clapham presented this inventory and appraisement which was OR.

Pages 138-40. Inventory of estate of John Ashmore. dec.
 Includes 6 negroes valued at £ 79.0.0.
 Total valuation £ 144.0.3.
 Made 25 Nov. 1737.   Leo Barker
        William Farrow
        Joseph Davis
Mary (M) Ashmore signed the inventory.
28 Nov. 1737. Mary Ashmore returned this inventory and appraisement which was OR.

Page 140. A supplementary inventory of the goods of Thos. Triplet, made 24 June 1737.
 To one negro woman named Patt £ 20.0.0
        Thos. Lewis
        Robt. Stephens

1737/38

28 Nov. 1737. Hugh West returned this supplemental inventory and appraismt. which was OR.

Pages 140-41. Bond of Ann Mason and Jeremiah Bronaugh unto Denis McCarty, Gent., justice. For £ 50. 27 Feb. 1737. Ann Mason is admx. of Richard Deacin, dec.

         Ann Mason
         Jera. Bronaugh

Wit: John Bowie
27 Feb. 1737. Ack. and OR.

Pages 142-43. Bond of Amos Janney and Lewis Elzey, Gent., unto Denis McCarty, Gent., justice. For £ 50. 27 Feb. 1737. Amos Janney is admr. of Joseph Tindall.

         Amos Janney
         Lewis Elzey

Wit: John Bowie
27 Feb. 1737. Ack. and OR.

Pages 143-44. Will of William Debell, dated 14 Nov. 1737.
 William Dibell of Prince William County of Virginia, planter, being very sick and weak in body.
 Unto Margret my derly bloued wife three catle, a hars and a mear and a beed and a poat and one dish and three plats.
 I give to my well beloved son William Debell three catle one hars, one beed and my gun, one pan, one dish and three pleats and himself to be free at eighteen years of age.
 My brother Joseph Debell whom I likways constut my whol and sol exactor of this my last will and Testment.
 I likways will and allaw that if it would pleas God to call William Debel from hence without haer that all his afacts shall to his mother fall.
Wit: William (M) Debell
John Gladin
Samuel Mackinly
 I do hereby sartifee that I the exeter of this will and Testement of Wm. Debell doe give up all my right and title of the Excetership to the widow named Margrat Debell and dont intend to truble my self any furder in the Eafair as Wittness my hand this 27th day of Febr. 1737.
Wit: Joseph Debell
Mathewis [sic]
Saml. McKinly
 27 March 1738. Proved by oaths of witnesses. Joseph Debell the exr. herein named relinquished his right to Margaret Debell widow and relict of the testator, who is granted letters of administration.

Pages 144-45. Bond of Margaret Debell, Nicholas Grimes, John Gladwin and Solomon Organ unto Denis McCarty, Gent., justice. For £ 50. 27 March 1738. Margaret Debell is admx. with the will annexed of William Debell, dec.

         Margaret (M) Debell
         Nicholas (N) Grimes
         John Gladdin
Wit: Jno. Bowie   Solomon Orgain
27 March 1738. Ack. and OR.

Page 146. Bond of Ralph Hughs and Thomas Conway unto the Worshipful Justices of Prince William County. For £ 100.
27 March 1738. Ralph Hughes is guardian of James Gardiner, orphan.
          Ralph (R H) Hughes
          Thomas Conway
 Wit: Jno. Bowie.
 27 March 1738. Ack. and OR.

Page 147. The estate of Matthew Organ, dec. [tobo.] [£]
 To funeral expences per himself   500
 To funeral expences per his wife   500
 To funeral expences for Edwd. Hagan an
  orphan under his care   200
 To paid Jeremh. Bronaugh per Rect.   1208
 To paid Mr. Benj. Tasker   13.18. 4½
 Solomon Organ, administrator.
 28 March 1738. Account allowed and OR.

Page 148. Inventory of estate of Wm. Debells, dec., made in obedience to order of 27 March 1738.
 Total valuation £ 19.3.0.
         Geo. Harrison
         Wm. Hale
         Hugh West
 Margt. Debell, administratrix.
 24 April 1738. Margaret Debell returned this inventory and appraisemt. which was admitted to record.

Pages 148-49. Will of Sarah Parker, dated 27 Nov. 1737.
 Sarah Parker of Hambleton Parish in the County of Prince William being very sick and weak in body.
 To Ann Lucas one gold ring, one silver lacehatt [?], also one thousand pounds of tobacco.
 To Mary Ashmore, one pair of silver shooe clasps.
 To Francis Purnell, son of John Chapman Purnell and Elizabeth his wife, all the rest of my goods and chattels to be paid him at the age of twenty one years.
 Also I make ordain constitute and appoint John Chapman Purnell executor of this my last will and testament.
Wit: Sarah (S P) Parker
Mary (M) Ashmore
Elizabeth Hargess
Simon Lutterell
 24 April 1738. Proved by the oaths of Mary Ashmore and Simon Luttrell two of the witnesses thereto. On motion of John Chapman Purnell executor herein named and his performing what is usual in such cases, certificate was granted him for obtaining a probate.

Pages 149-50. Bond of John Chapman Purnell, Francis Lucas and Thomas Chapman unto Denis McCarty, justice. For £ 150.
24 April 1738. John Chapman Purnel is exor. of Sarah Parker, dec.
         John Chapman Purnel
         Franc. (F) Lucas
 Wit: Jno. Bowie   Thomas Chapman
 24 April 1738. Ack. and OR.

1738

Pages 150-52. Inventory and appraisement of estate of Robert Alexander, Gent., dec., made by order of 24 April 1738.
    Includes 8 negroes valued at £ 124.0.0.
    One servt. man David Kelly   £ 6.0.0
    Total valuation £ 162.4.0
    And did likewise set apart the widow's third and divide the same between the legatees as followeth:
    The Widow's Part   £ 54. 1.4
    Jane Alexander's Part   31. 8.0
    Gerrard Alexander   20.14.8
    17 May 1738
                            Wm. Henry Terret
                            Geo. Harrison
                            Thom. Pearson

    22 May 1738. Thomas Pearson returned this division of the estate of Robert Alexander, dec., which was OR.

Page 152. Inventory and appraisement of estate of James Henderson, dec., made in obedience to order of 26 Sept. 1737. Appraisers sworn before Mr. William Hackney, Gent.
    Includes 299 acres of land at £ 12.0.0
    Total valuation £ 14.1.2
                            Jos. Right
                            Charles Backer
                            Charles Taylor

    25 May 1738. Jeffery Johnson returned this inventory and appraisement which was OR.

Page 153. An additional inventory and appraisement of the estate of John Walker, dec.   3 May 1738.
    Total valuation £ 5.11.-
                            John Gregg
                            Stephn. Delisle
                            William Farrow

    23 May 1738. Leonard Barker presented this additional inventory which was OR.

Page 153. Will of John Edge, dated 16 July 1737.
    John Edge of the County of Prince William in Virginia being very sick and week in body.
    Unto Rachel Spiller wife of William Spiller Jun. one negro lad called Harry and one negro woman named Ginny enduring her natural life and at her decese then it is my will that my kinswoman Elizabeth Maguire shall have the said two negros Harry and Ginny her and her heirs forever but if the said negro woman should have any children that then the said Rachel Spillar shall have the Disposal of the said negro children to give to whomsoever she pleases.
    To Rachel Spiller all the rest of my personal estate be it of what kind, nature or quality soever enduring the natural life of the said Rachel Spillar and after her decease to my kinswoman Elizabeth Maguire who is now bound to William and Rachel Spillar and to her and her heirs forever.
    I do hereby constitute and appoint my loving friend Rachel Spiller to be my sole executrix of this my last will

and testament.
Wit: John (X) Edge
Lewis Tackett
Mary (X) Tackett
Francis Lacon [?]
   26 June 1738. Presented in Court by Rachel Spiller the executrix within named. Proved by the oaths of the witnesses.

Page 154. Bond of Rachel Spiller, Francis Lacen [?] and Lewis Talbert unto John Colvill, justice. For £ 60. 26 June 1738. Rachel Spiller is extx. of John Edge, dec.
                          Rachel Spiller
                          Fran. Lacen [?]
                          Lewis Tackett
   Wit: John Bowie
   26 June 1738. Ack. and OR.

Page 155. Inventory and appraisement of estate of John Edge, dec., made in obedience to order of 26 June 1738. Appraisers sworn before Thomas Harrison, Gent., justice.
   Includes 3 negroes valued at £ 42.
   Total valuation £ 55.19.6
   An inventory of the estate of John Edge Deced. taken and appraised by Rachel Spiller
                        Matthew (X) Moss
                        James Bland
                        William (W) Thorn
   11 July 1738. The above named apprairs. sworn before me
                        Thos. Harrison Jun.
   24 July 1738. Rachel Spiller presented this inventory and appraisement which was OR.

Page 156. Inventory and appraisement of estate of John Davis, dec., made in obedience to order of 26 June 1738.
   Includes 1 negro man valued at £ 25.
   Total valuation £ 56.3.-
   An inventory of the estate of John Davis taken and apprais'd by Margt. Davis.
                        Timothy Tharton [?]
                        Peter Glascock
                        John Glascock
   21 July 1738. The above appraisers sworn before me
                        Tho. Harrison Junr.
   24 July 1738. Margaret Davis presented this inventory and appraisement which was OR.

Pages 157-58. Bond of Margaret Davis, John Purcel and Owen Lard unto John Colvill, Gent., justice. For £ 100. 26 June 1738. Margaret Davis is admx. of John Davis, dec.
                        Margaret (X) Davis
                        John Purcell
                        Owen Lard
   26 June 1738. Ack. and OR.

Pages 158-59. Bond of Sarah Lambert, William Champe and John Reeves unto Denis McCarty, Gent., justice. For £ 50. 28 Aug. 1738. Sarah Lambert is admx. of Joseph Lambert, dec.

1738/39

> Sarah (X) Lambert
> William Champe
> John Reve

Wit: Jno. Bowie
28 Aug. 1738. Ack. and OR.

Pages 159-60. Bond of Richard Blackburn, Benjamin Grayson and John Gregg unto the Worshipful Justices of Prince William County. For £ 1200. 26 Sept. 1738. Richard Blackburn is guardian of William Elliot, orphan.
> R. Blackburn
> Benja. Grayson
> John Gregg

Wit: Jno. Bowie, Catesby Cocke
26 Sept. 1738. Ack. and OR.

Page 160. Inventory of Lampers estate. Appreset by Nimrod Hot and George Calvert and Murris Veal.
Total valuation £ 5.10.-
> Nimrod Hot
> George (G C) Calvert
> Murris (M V) Veal

27 Nov. 1738. Sarah Lambert presented this inventory and appraisement which was OR.

Page 160. Joseph Lamport Estate
Account signed by Sara Lampert
27 Nov. 1738. This account was allowed by the Court and OR.

Page 161. Bond of Maurice Veals and Richard Blackburn unto Worshipful Justices of Prince William County. For £ 200. 27 Nov. 1738. Maurice Veal is guardian of Thomas Arrington, orphan.
> Maurice (M) Veal
> R. Blackburn

Wit: Jno. Bowie
27 Nov. 1738. Ack. and OR.

Pages 161-62. Will of Joseph Buchanan, dated 23 Nov. 1738.
Joseph Buchanan of Prince Wm. County and Parish of Hamilton being sick and weak in body.
To my loving wife Elizabeth Buchanan all my estate both real and personal during her natural life or widowhood and after that my moveables to be equally divided amongst my children, my land to be equally divided amongst my sons (Vizt) John Buchanan, Joseph Buchanan, Neavill Buchanan, Wm. Buchanan George Buchanan, all to be distributed by my loving wife as aforesd. whom I make and ordain as my whole and sole executrix together with my loving brothers Georg Neavill and Joseph Minter my executors.
Wit:
> Joseph Buchanan

Thomas Davies
Ester (X) Stone
Judith (X) Davies
26 Feb. 1738. Presented in Court by Elizabeth Buchanan the executrix. Proved by the oaths of the witnesses.

Pages 162-63. Bond of Elizabeth Buchanan, George Nevil and Joseph Minter unto Denis McCarty, Gent., Justice. For ₤ 300. 26 Feb. 1738. Elizabeth Buchanan is extx. of Joseph Buchanan.
         Elizabeth (E) Buchanan
         George Neavill
         Joseph Minter
 Wit: Jno. Bowie
 26 Feb. 1738. Ack. and OR.

Pages 163-64. Bond of Anne Lucas, Richard Higgins and Francis Searson unto Denis McCarty, Gent., justice. For ₤ 100. 26 Feb. 1738. Anne Lucas is admx. of Francis Lucas, dec.
         Anne (X) Lucas
         Richard (R) Higgins
         Fras. Searson
 Wit: Jno. Bowie
 26 Feb. 1738. Ack. and OR.

Pages 164-65. Bond of Margaret Anderton, Stephen Martin and Thomas Reno unto Denis McCarty, Gent., justice. For ₤ 100. 26 Feb. 1738. Margaret Anderton is admx. of Richard Anderton.
         Margaret (X) Anderton
         Stephen Martin
         Thomas Reno
 Wit: Jno. Bowie
 26 Feb. 1738. Ack. and OR.

Pages 165-66. Bond of James Harbert, George Pimmet [?] and William Brewster unto Denis McCarty, Gent., justice. For ₤ 200. 26 Feb. 1738. James Harbert is admr. of John Queen, dec.
         James Harbert
         George (X) Pimmet [?]
         Wm. Brewster
 Wit: Jno. Bowie
 26 Feb. 1738. Ack. and OR.

Page 167. The estate of James Henderson, dec.   [₤]
 To pd. Thomas Jackson by Judgmt. from Mr.
  Hackney   0.15. 0
 To Do paid Jacob Holsclaw   0. 4. 6
 To a Lawyers fee at Spotswoods suit   -.15. -
         Jeffery Johnson, exr.
 28 Feb. 1738. This account was regulated by the Court.

Pages 167-68. Inventory and appraisement of estate of Francis Luckus, dec. 17 March 1738/9.
 No total valuation given.
         Leo Barker
         John Carr
         Wm. Farrow
 26 March 1739. Anne Lucas returned this inventory and appraisement which was OR.

Pages 168-69. Bond of Mary Davis, Richard Higgins and Thomas Reno unto Denis McCarty, Gent., justice. For ₤ 50. 26 March 1739. Mary Davis is admx. of Richard Davis, dec.

                              Mary (M) Davis
                              Richard (R) Higgins
                              Thom. Reno
Wit: Jno. Bowie
26 March 1739. Ack. and OR.

Pages 169-70. Bond of John Garner, Humphrey Pope and Thomas Reno unto Worshl. Justices of Prince William County. For ₤ 200. 26 Feb. 1738. John Garner is guardian of Charles Garner, orphan.
                              John Garner
                              Hum. Pope
                              Thoms. Reno
Wit: Jno. Bowie
26 Feb. 1738. Ack. and ordered to be certified.
26 March 1739. OR.

Pages 170-71. Appraisement of estate of Joseph Buchanan, dec., made in pursuance to order of 26 February.
    Includes 4 negroes valued at ₤ 95.
    Total valuation ₤ 163.1.11½
                              Val Barton
                              Thos. Davies
                              Richd. Jarvis
    Elizabeth (E) Buchanan signed the inventory.
    28 May 1739. Elizabeth Buchanan returned this inventory and appraisement which was OR.

Pages 172-73. Inventory and appraisement of estate of Richd. Anderton, dec., made in obedience to order of 26 Feb. 1738.
    Total valuation ₤ 34.6.-, plus 5 sh.
                              Val Barton
                              Antho. Seale
                              John Diskin
    Margt. (X) Anderton, admx.
    28 May 1739. Margaret Anderton returned this inventory and appraisment which was OR.

Page 173. Richard Anderton, dec.   1739.
    Margt. Camell signed the account.
    28 May 1739. This account was regulated by the Court.

Page 174. Bond of John Kinchelo, John Diskin and Valentine Peyton unto the Worshipful Justices of Prince William County. For ₤ 300. 28 May 1739. John Kinchelo is guardian of Mary, Anne and Margaret Osborn (orphans of Thomas Osborn, dec.)
                              John (John) Kinchelo
                              John Diskin
                              Val Peyton
Wit: Jno. Bowie.
28 May 1739. Ack. and OR.

Page 174-75. Bond of Elizabeth Neale, Francis Awbrey, Gent., and John Sturman unto Denis McCarty, Gent., justice. For ₤ 500. 28 May 1739. Elizabeth Neale is admx. of John Neale, dec.

                                    Elizabeth Neale
                                    Fras. Awbrey
                                    Jno. Sturman
Wit: Jno. Bowie
28 May 1739. Ack. and OR.

Pages 175-76. Appraisement of estate of Richard Davis, made pursuant to order of 26 March 1738/9.
Total valuation ₤ 34.2.8.
                                    Isaac Farguson
                                    John Burdett
                                    Thomas Leachman
25 June 1739. Mary Davis returned this inventory and appraisement which was OR.

Pages 176-78. Will of Edward Sute, dated 13 April 1739.
Edward Sute of the Parish of Hamilton and County of Prince William, planter, being sick and weak of body.
To my loving wife Elizabeth Sute the use, labour and occupation of my man slave Cupid for and during her natural life and after her decease I give devise and bequeath the sd. slave to my beloved daughter Margaret Sute and her heirs forever.
To my sd. daughter Margaret my negro female slave Sarah and her issue.
To my beloved daughter Mary Sute a negro child named Jamie the son of negro Sarah.
All my stock of hogs and cattle, all the mony now in my possession and all other goods and chattels and all my estate whither Real or personal (being first converted into mony) to be equally divided amongst my wife and my daughter Margaret and my daughter Mary abovementioned.
I hereby nominate constitute appoint and ordain my trusty and beloved friends Thomas Harrison Junr. and Benjamin Bullet Gent. my sole and whole exrs. to this my last will and testament. I also appoint them the sd. Thomas Harrison junr. and Benjamin Bullet to be guardians to my abovementioned beloved daughters till they shall arrive at the age of fourteen years.
Wit: Edward (X) Sute
Ja. Keith, Rot. Stephen
Susu. (X) Johnson, Aron Drummond
25 June 1739. Presented in Court by Thomas Harrison Junr. and Benjamin Bullet the executors therein named. Proved by the oaths of the witnesses.

Pages 178-79. Bond of Thomas Harrison, Junr., Benjamin Bullet, James Keith and John McMillian unto Denis McCarty, Gent., justice. For ₤ 200. 25 June 1739. Thomas Harrison Junr. and Benjamin Bullet are exors. of Edward Sute.
                                    Thos. Harrison Junr.
                                    Benja. Bullet
                                    Ja. Keith
                                    John (I) McMillian
Wit: Jno. Bowie
25 June 1739. Ack. and OR.

Pages 179-80. Bond of John Brown and Richard Osborn unto Denis McCarty, Gent., justice. For £ 50. 23 July 1739. John Brown is admr. of James Gil, dec.

          John Brown
          Richard Osborn

Wit: Jno. Bowie
23 July 1739. Ack. and OR.

Pages 180-81. Will of Catherine Padderson, dated 21 May 1739.
 Catherine Padderson being sick and weak in body.
 Unto my well beloved son Elixander Going one negro man named Robin and one horse and a horse colt and one cow and calf and a cow yearlin and halph of my movable household stuf and one parcel of land whereon I now live containing sixty six acres it being part of a tract containing one hundred and thirty two acres.
 Unto my well beloved daghter Susannah Going one negro man named Jackey and one mare and saddle cow and calf and two cow yearlins and one feather bed and bolster, a rugg and one pare of blankits and halph the houshold stuf.
 My crop of tob: which is now in my house after my debts is paid I bequeath to be equally divided between my son Elixander Going and my daughter Susanna Going.
 I leave my well beloved son John Going whole and sole executor of this my last will and testament.
Wit: Catherin (O) Padderson
Tho. Ford
Jane Ford
Ann Gladding
 23 July 1739. Presented in Court by John Going sole executor herein named who prayed certificate for obtaining a probate thereof but it being suggested that the deceds. husband is living on the motion of the said John Going and giving security for his just and faithfull administration of the said deceds. estate certificate is granted him for obtaining letters of administration.

Pages 181-82. Bond of John Going, William Scutt and John Hollis unto Denis McCarty, Gent., justice. For £ 100. 23 July 1739. John Going is admr. of Catherine Padderson, dec.
          John (I) Going
          John (H) Hollis
          William (X) Scutt

Wit: Jno. Bowie
23 July 1739. Ack. and OR.

Pages 182-83. Appraisement of estate of Jon. Neale, dec., made in obedience to order of 28 May 1739. Appraisers sworn before Fras. Awbrey, Gent.
 Includes 8 negroes valued at £ 86.
 Total valuation £ 121.11.6.
          Richd. Wheeler
          John Stroughn
          John Evans

Eliza. Neale, admx.
 23 July 1739. John Awbrey, Gent., presented this inventory and appraisment which was OR.

Pages 183-84. Inventory of John Queens, dec., Estate.
  Includes 2 negroes valued at £ 29.
  Total valuation £ 60.4.-
                              Guy Broadwater
                              Edward (E) Ems
                              John (I) Tramell
James Harbert, admr.
23 July 1739. James Harbert returned this inventory and appraisment which was OR.

Pages 184-85. Inventory of estate of Edward Sute, 18 July 1739.
  Includes 3 negroes valued at £ 51.
  Total valuation £ 92.18.-
                              John Overall
                              William Whitledge
                              John Glascock
  The above named appraisers sworn before me as ye law direct.
18 July 1739.   Thos. Harrison Junr.
  23 July 1739. Benjamin Bullet returned this inventory and appraisment which was OR.

Page 185. The remainder of the estate of James Henderson, dec., apraised.
  Total valuation £ 0.7.0 and 190 pounds of tobacco.
                              Jos. Right
                              Charles Backer [Barker?]
                              Charles Taylor
  24 July 1739. Jeffery Johnson returned this additional inventory which was OR.

Page 186. Estate of James Henderson, dec.   [£]
  To Ballance of Jacob Holzclaw's accot. proved
     before Wm. Hackney Gent.   -. 4. 7
  To Thomas Jackmans account proved before do.   -.15. -
  Jeffery Johnson, exor.
  24 July 1739. Jeffery Johnson presented this account which was allowed and OR.

Page 186. To be added to the inventory of Joseph Buchanan, dec.
  Total valuation £ 3 and 4545 pounds of tobacco.
                              Thos. Davies
                              Richd. Jarvis
  Eliza. (E) Buchanan signed the inventory
  27 Aug. 1739. Elizabeth Buchanan returned this additional inventory which was OR.

Pages 186-87. Bond of Elizabeth Duncan, Daniel Trammel and John Burk unto Denis McCarty, Gent., justice. For £ 50.
27 Aug. 1739. Elizabeth Duncan is admx. of John Duncan.
                              Elizabeth (X) Duncan
                              Daniel (X) Trammel
                              John (B) Burk
  Wit: Jno. Bowie
  27 Aug. 1739. Ack. and OR.

1739

Page 188. Inventory of part of the estate of William Debells, dec.
   Total valuation ℒ 3.12.0.
                                    Geo. Harrison
                                    Hugh West
   Margt. McKenley signed the inventory.
   27 Aug. 1739. Margaret McKinley returned this additional inventory which was OR.

Page 188. Inventory of the estate of Catherine Padderson.
   Includes 2 negro men valued at ℒ 25.0.0
   Total valuation ℒ 36.2.4 3/4
   27 Aug. 1739   Thos. Ford
                                    Thos. Elzey
                                    Richard Simpson
   John (X) Going, admr.
   27 Aug. 1739. John Going presented this inventory and appraisment which was OR.

Page 189. Bond of Elizabeth Broadwater, John Turley and Valentine Peyton unto Worshipful Justices of Prince William County. For ℒ 200. 27 Aug. 1739. Elizabeth Broadwater is guardian of Charles Broadwater, orphan.
                                    Elizabeth (X) Broadwater
                                    John Turley
                                    Val Peyton
   Wit: Jno. Bowie
   27 Aug. 1739. Ack. and OR.

Pages 189-90. Inventory of the estate of John Duncan, dec., made in obedience to order of 27 Aug. 1739.
   Total valuation ℒ 18.6.6
                                    Sampson Darrell
                                    John Musgrove
                                    Henry Tailor
   Elizabeth Duncan, admx.
   24 Sept. 1739. Elizabeth Duncan returned this inventory and appraisment which was OR.

Pages 190-93. 1737. The estate of Thomas Osborne deceased to John Champe.   [tobo.]   [ℒ]
   To paid Frans. Lucas his share of crop
      at Bull run   1366
   To paid Colo. Carter for Emanuel Underwood   724
   To paid Capt. Whitfield   600
   To paid Mr. John Wilson   1660
   To paid Richard Tilley by Acct. proved   280
   To paid William Dent by Acct. proved   389
   To paid Mr. Thos. Harrison for Levys &c   838
   To paid John Kenchelo by Acct.   352
   To paid William Slade for his share of
      the crop at Cedar Run   854
   To paid the cost of Peter Kerrs Judgement   91
   To paid Mr. Diskin   98
   To paid John Tayloe Esqr. his note of hand   750   43. 7. 6
   To paid Isaac Farguson per Acct.   400

To paid George Goring per Acct. proved	365	
To paid Jno. Allen and Thos. Young for fees	364	
To paid John Canterbury for boarding two children till last Christmas	500	
To paid Richard Osbornes Acct.	144	
To paid Mr. Blackburn for Henry Washington	140	
To paid Mr. Jno. Gregg as per his Acct. for publick dues &c for 1737	549	
To paid Henry Cooper per Acct.	280	
To Mr. Cocks Clerks note	100	
To paid Emanuel Underwood for freedom dues and one years schooling	600	
To paid Mr. Edward Barry per acct.	257	
To paid Henry Murphy per acct.	100	
To paid William West per acct.	600	
To paid Thomas Young for fees	27	
To paid Frans. Lucas for his share of crop at Bull Run for the year 1737	350	
To paid James Coburne for his share of Cedar run crop 1737	720	
To paid Frans. Searson	20	
To paid Mr. Blackburne balance his tobo. acct.	54	
To paid Mr. Catesby Cock for fees	1774	
To paid Mr. John Gregg		3. 7.10
To paid Mr. John Grant		-.10. 2
To paid Duke Cannon by acct. proved		-. 2. -
To paid John Kencheloe by acct.		3.13. 9
To paid James Coburne by acct.		17. 6
To paid Peter Kerr per Judgment		35.10. 6
To paid James Jones by Acct.		3. 7½
To paid Geo. Gray for settling the Accts.		1. 6. -
To a Debt contracted with Doctr. Goodall wch. I never received		1.16. -
To paid James Frost by acct.		3. 9
To paid Mr. John Gregg		6. 8
To paid Mr. Anthony Seale Cash		5. 4
To paid Mr. Nicholl Boutine		3.14. 7
To paid Mosley Battalie Attorny		13.10. -
To paid Frans. Lucas		-.17. -
To paid Ditto		-.18. 4
To paid Qts. of 1105 acres of land		1. 7. 7
To paid James Cork per acct.		-. 3. -
To paid Lucas for his share of corn for the year 1737		2. -. -
To paid Moses Congrove per acct.		-. 5. -
To paid Mrs. Ashmore per acct.		-. 6. -
To your balance due Lyde and Cooper		2.14. 9½
25 per cent on Ditto		12.10
To paid Mr. Falkners acct.		4.17. -½
To paid George Blackmore per acct. and proved		1. -. -
To paid Mr. Diskin for his pr. Inspectrs. notes		-. 3. 9
To paid Mr. Cock for fees for 1738	763	
To paid Mr. Tyler Clerk of Stafford	233	

1739

        To paid Mr. Grant for defective Quit Rents   21.14. 2½
1737. Per Contra
    By recd. of Capt. Harrison at Sundry
        times to the first of November   28570
    By an allowance on the Goods bot. in
        company with Mr. Blackburne   1375
    By Thos. Stribling   622
    By John Canterbury   1340
    By James Coburne   81
    By 5 hhds. of Edwd. Graham and Thos.
        Waters wth. Cask   4488
    By Lenord Holms   535
    By Mr. John Gregg   191
    By James Coburnes Bill   200
    By recd. of Thos. Young for sundry
        executions   3679   3. 5. -
    By John Kencheloe for Robt. Taylor   270
    By Mr. Blackburne balance his Cash acct.   -. 4.10
    By Do for Danl. Diskins Execution   358   1. 5. 3
    By Charles Grimes   686
    By John Grimes   1. 5. -
    By Mr. Payton   -.11. 4
    By James French   1. -. 5
    By Moses Linton and Robt. Jones   1. 5. 6
    By Mr. Ralph Falkner   5.19.11½
    By one sword sold Mr. Cock   3.10. -
    By William Bayley   11. 7. 3
    By George Calvert   13.10. 9
    By sundry effects as was pack'd up at Mr.
        John Kencheloes and sent round per the
        new sloop exclusive of the waring
        apparell   10. -. -
    By John Allen for Charles Taylor   546
    By ballance Gibsons execution   810
    By Bristows debt   298
    By recd. of John Sturman in pr. of his
        execution   13. 1. 2
    By Thos. Striblings ballance   235
    By John Young   301
    By John Young   150
    By notes of Mr. Harrison to pay West and
        Murfitt   700
    By Saml. Farmers Exo.   841
    24 Sept. 1739. John Champe, Gent., Admr. of Thomas Osborne,
Gent., dec., presented this account which was OR.

Pages 194-95. 1738. The estate of Thomas Osborne, dec.
    Allotted Mrs. Osborne for her thirds and her childs
part Vizt. £ 98.14.7
    Effects left at Bull run Qr. under the care of Mr. Jno.
Kencheloe. £ 310.4.2½.
    24 Sept. 1739. John Champe, Gent., Admr. of Thomas Osborne,
Gent., dec., presented this account which was allowed and OR.

Page 195. An additional inventory of the estate of Catherine
Padderson, dec. 26 Nov. 1739.

Total valuation ₤ 1.1.-.
Tho. Ford
Tho. Elzey
Richard Simson

Jno. (X) Going signed the inventory.
26 Nov. 1739. John Going returned this additional inventory and appraisment which was OR.

Pages 195-96. Will of Elinor Sanders, dated 31 Oct. 1739.
Elenor Sanders of Prince William County being sick and weak in bead.
Unto my sister Rebecker Grifeth one gold ring and three chests.
To my daughter Elinor Vilett on Cloack and a white gound, one duble gound and one manttle.
Unto my daughter Margarett Hyde one feather bead and rugg and pr. of Blankets, six pewter plates, two pewter dishes, one gound and petticoate of Callemenkco [?] one pair of cottin stockins, one suite pinners, one pr. of gloves and holland shift and one mear and one lase hatt.
To my daughter Elizabeth Hairs one old feather bead, one old rugg, one blanket, one gound and petticoate of cottin stuff, one holland shift, one apin, one suite of head cloaths, one iron pott.
Unto my daughter Mary Sanders one gound and peticoate of camletteens, also one quilted peticoate, one side sadle, one holland shift.
Unto my son Hundley Elder one shilling current money.
Unto my daughter Jemimy Elder two whestcoats, one shift and two pr. of shews as Johnson owes me.
The rest of my estate I leave to be divided equally amongst my children.
I make ordain and appoint my son in law Edward Vilett whole and sole executor of this my last will and testament.
Wit: Elinor (X) Sanders
Charles (C D) Grifeth
John (T) Tramell
Zepha Wade
27 Nov. 1739. Presented in Court and proved by the oaths of the witnesses thereto and admitted to record. Then Edward Vilett the Exr. therein named refused the burthen of the executorship and on the motion of Charles Griffith and his giving security certificate was granted him for obtaining letters of administration with the will annexed.

Page 197. Bond of Charles Griffeth and Edward Vilet unto Denis McCarty, Gent., justice. For ₤ 100. 27 Nov. 1739. Charles Griffith is admr. of Elinor Sanders.
Charles (C D) Griffith
Edward (X) Vilet

Wit: Jno. Bowie
27 Nov. 1739. Ack. and OR.

Pages 198-99. Bond of Hester Hampton, Christopher Johnson and Gabriel Adams, Junr., unto Denis McCarty, Gent., justice. For ₤ 50. 27 Nov. 1739. Hester Hampton is admx. of Joseph

1739/40, 1738 [?]   47

Hampton, dec.
                              Hester (E) Hampton
                              Christopher (C) Johnson
                              Gabriel (X) Adams, Junr.
    Wit: Jno. Bowie
    27 Nov. 1739. Ack. and OR.

Page 199. 1739. The estate of Catherine Pattison, dec.
    To 2 levs. pd. Edwd. Barry   116 [tobo.]
    To pd. Capt. Val Peyton   364
    To pd. Thomas Ford   40
    To pd. Alexander Gowin   330
    To pd. Susanna Gowin   250
    To bal. due per John Gowin   468
    To pd. Mr. Wm. Dunlop   ₺ 7. 4. -
    John (X) Gowin signed the account.
    27 Nov. 1739. John Going presented this account which was
allowed and OR.

Page 200. 1736. The orphans of Wansford Arrington
Dr Thos. and Sarah Arrington   [tobo.]   [₺]
    To Sundry goods bought of Richd. Blackburn
         and myself   2517
    1738. To sundry goods of Benjn. Grayson 515
    To sundry goods of John Grayham   395
    To sundry goods of Rd. Blackburn   89
    1736. By Mr. John Gregg for hire of slave
         named Will   900
    By 1 years rent of Wm. Frankham   530
    1737.
    By rent from Wm. Frankham   365   -. 5. 6
    By two several payments of Thos. Bristoes
         rent   590
    25 Nov. 1738. Signed by James Mus
    27 Nov. 1738. James Muse guardian of Thomas Arrington
presented this account which was OR.

Pages 200-01. Harrison's account against Clark.
    1738. To pd. James Storey   ₺ -. 6. -
    Geo. Harrison signed the account.
    27 Nov. 1738. George Harrison guardian of Susana Clark
presented this account which was OR.

Pages 201-02. Bond of Daniel McCarty, Denis McCarty and
Lawrence Washington unto John Colvill, Gent., justice. For
₺ 2000. 25 Feb. 1739. Daniel McCarty is admr. of William
Dunlop, dec.   Danl. McCarty
                              Denis McCarty
                              Lawr. Washington
    Wit: Jno. Bowie
    25 Feb. 1739. Ack. and OR.

Pages 202-03. Bond of William Foster and John Diskin unto
Denis McCarty, Gent., justice. For ₺ 100. 25 Feb. 1739.
William Foster is admr. of Richard Miller, dec.

                                    Wm. (M) Foster
                                    John Diskin
Wit: Jno. Bowie
25 Feb. 1739. Ack. and OR.

Pages 203-05. Bond of Anne Barton, William Foster and Richard Jarvis unto Denis McCarty, Gent., justice. For ₤ 100. 25 Feb. 1739. Ann Barton is admx. of Valentine Barton, dec.
                                    Anne (A) Barton
                                    Willm. (M) Foster
                                    Richd. Jarvis
    Wit: Jno. Bowie.
    25 Feb. 1739. Ack. and OR.

Pages 205-06. Inventory of the estate of Ellioner Sanders made according to an order of 27 Nov. 1739. Appraised this 19 Feb. 1739 per us Richard Osborn, Wm. Payne, John Manley.
    Total valuation ₤ 19.19.3.
    Charles Griffoth, admr.
    25 Feb. 1739. Charles Griffith presented this inventory and appraisment which was OR.

Pages 206-07. Bond of John McKenny, George Taylor and Henry Taylor unto Denis McCarty, Gent., justice. For ₤ 50. 25 Feb. 1739. John McKenny is admr. of Nicholas Richardson, dec.
                                    John (X) McKenny
                                    Geo. Taylor
                                    Henry (H) Taylor
    Wit: Jno. Bowie
    25 Feb. 1739. Ack. and OR.

Pages 207-08. Bond of Richard Osborn and Daniel French, Junr., unto Denis McCarty, Gent., justice. For ₤ 50. 25 Feb. 1739. Richard Osborn is admr. of William Sleming.
                                    Richd. Osborn
                                    Daniel French
    Wit: Jno. Bowie
    25 Feb. 1739. Ack. and OR.

Pages 208-09. 1735. The estate of Walter Griffin Dr. to Lewis Elzey.   [tobo.]   [₤]
    To paid Richard Simson   200
    To paid John Peek   50
    To paid Thomas Harrison, Junr.   35
    To paid Thomas Barnett   100
    To paid Randall Holbrook   150
    To paid Ann Rigg   200
    To paid Ebenezer Moss   -.13. 6
    To paid Ann Scandall   -. 5. -
    To paid Arthur Neal   2.10. -
    To paid French Mason   -. 9. 9
    To paid Rosanah Hulet her freedom dues   2. 8. -
    To paid James Halley   1. -. -
    To a fee paid Mr. John Mercer   -.15. -
    27 Feb. 1739. Lewis Elzey, Gent., exhibited this account which was allowed and OR.

1739/40

Pages 209-10. Bond of Mary Taylor and John Wood unto Denis McCarty, Gent., justice. For ₤ 100. 24 March 1739. Mary Taylor is admx. of Charles Taylor.
                                          Mary Taylor
                                          John (I) Wood
Wit: John Bowie
24 March 1739. Ack. and OR.

Pages 210-11. Appraisment of estate of Richd. Millers, dec., made pursuant to order of 24 Feb. 1739.
   Total valuation ₤ 21.15.1¼.
                                          Antho. Seale
                                          Richd. Jarvis
                                          John Dawkins
Willm. (W) Foster signed the inventory.
24 March 1739. William Foster returned this inventory and appraisment and it was OR.

Pages 211-12. Will of Edward Young, dated 22 Jan. 1739/40.
   Edward Young in the back woods of Prince Willm. County, Virginia, being very sick and weak in body.
   To Mary my dearly beloved wife whom I likewise constitute make and ordain my only and sole executor of this my last will and testament all and singular my lands, mesuages and teniments by her freely to be possessed and injoyed during her natural life excepting one gun I give to my beloved son Daniell Young with all my carpenters and shooe makers tools and all other my real and personal estate to be in her own full power and disposall at her discease.
Wit: Edward (X) Young
John Bailey
Jacob (I) Smith
Robt. (R C) Colcklow
   24 March 1739. Proved by the oaths of John Bailey and Jacob Smith, two of the witnesses thereto. Certificate is granted Mary Young for obtaining a probate.

Pages 212-13. Bond of Mary Young, John Young Constable and Jacob Smith unto Denis McCarty, Gent., justice. For ₤ 100. 24 March 1739. Mary Young is extx. of Edward Young.
                                        Mary (X) Young
                                        John Young const.
                                        Jacob (I) Smith

Wit: Jno. Bowie
24 March 1739. Ack. and OR.

Page 213. The estate of Richard Millers.
   Account for years 1737, 1738, 1739.
   24 March 1739.
   Willm. Foster signed the account.
   24 March 1739. William Foster exhibited this account which was allowed and OR.

Pages 214-15. Bond of Anne Guess, Thomas Ford and Richard Drakeford unto Denis McCarty, Gent., justice. For ₤ 300. 24 March 1739. Anne Guess is admx. of Joseph Guess, dec.

                            Anne (X) Guess
                            Tho. Ford
                            Richd. (R D) Drakeford
Wit: Jno. Bowie
24 March 1739. Ack. and OR.

Page 215. Bond of Charles Baker, Charles Wright and Jeoffery Johnson unto the Worshipful Justices of Prince William County. For ₤ 300. 24 March 1739. Charles Baker is guardian of Thomas Bullock, orphan.

                            Charles Baker
                            Charles (W) Wright
                            Jeoffery (X) Johnson
Wit: Jno. Bowie
24 March 1739. Ack. and OR.

Page 215. An inventory of the remainder of the estate of Edward Sute taken 20 March 1739/40.
    Total valuation ₤ 1.10.-
                            John Overall
                            John Glascock
                            Willm. Whitledge
The above appraisers sworn before me
                    Thos. Harrison, Junr.   20 March 1739/40.
    24 March 1739. Thomas Harrison, Junr., returned this additional inventory which was OR.

Pages 116-17. Will of John Holmes, dated 2 Feb. 1732/3.
    John Holms of Hamilton Parish in Prince William Coty. and Colony of Virga. being sick and weak in body.
    To my loving son James Holmes one hundred and fourteen acres of land (it being part of a greater tract of three hundred and forty acres lying upon the branches of Luckey Run and Johns Branch) to him and the heirs of his body lawfully begotten and for want of such heirs to my son Christopher Holmes and the heirs of his body lawfully begotten and for want of such heirs to my son Edmond Holmes and the heirs of his body lawfully begotten and for want of such to the next heir at law, my son James to have his part laid off (quantity and quality alike) where he is now seating.
    To my loving son Christopher Holmes one hundred and thirteen acres of land (it being part of the abovesaid greater tract) to him and the heirs of his body lawfully begotten and for want of such heirs to my son Edmund Holmes and the heirs of his body lawfully begotten and for want of such heirs to my son James Holmes and the heirs of his body lawfully begotten and for want of such to the next heir att law, my son Christopher to have his part laid off (quantity and quality alike) where he now lives.
    To my loving son Edmund Holmes (after the decease of my wife Mary Holmes) one hundred and thirteen acres of land it being the remainder of the abovesaid greater tract to him and the heirs of his body lawfully begotten and for want of such heirs to my son James Holmes and the heirs of his body lawfully begotten and for want of such heirs to my son Christopher Holmes and the heirs of his body lawfully begotten and for want

1739/40

of such to the next heir att law, my son Edmond to have the plantation where I now live, and his land laid off convenient to it, quantity and quality alike.
   To my loving wife Mary Holmes (whom I likewise appoint my only and sole executrix of this my last will and Testament) all my personal estate both within doors and without during her natural life and after her decease my will and desire is that my three sons before mentioned choose three men and they three men equally to divide it quantity and quality alike as near as possible amongst my three sons James, Christopher and Edmund Holmes.
Wit: John (J) Holmes
John Metcalfe
John Maden
John Whitledge
   24 March 1739. Presented in Court by Mary Holmes the executrix therein named. Proved by the oaths of the witnesses.

Pages 217-18. Bond of Mary Holmes, Christopher Holmes and John Whitledge unto Denis McCarty, Gent., justice. For ₤ 200. 24 March 1739. Mary Holmes is extx. of John Holmes, dec.
                              Mary (O) Holmes
                              Christopher (X) Holmes
                              John Whitledge
   Wit: Jno. Bowie
   24 March 1739. Ack. and OR.

Pages 218-19. Inventory of the estate of John Holmes, dec.
   No total valuation given.
   The above inventory taken by me the executrix of the above named estate.   Mary (O) Holmes
   24 March 1739. Mary Holmes presented this inventory and it was OR.

Pages 219-20. Disbursed on account of the estate of Richd. Anderton, dec., by Patrick Cambell the Succeedor. The tobacco at 12/6 pr. hundred.   [tobo.]   [₤]
   To Richard Blackburn for damages sustained
     in a bond of the estate   12. -. -
   To Dittos and. agt. the estate   3.18. 8
   To Ditto Judgt. agt. Do   337   2. 2. 1½
   To William Bailey his acct. agt. the estate   10.17. 7
   To Houseleys Judgment against Anderton   371   2. 6. 4½
   To Quit rents of 60 acres of land for the
     years 1735, 1736, 1737, 1738   58   -. 7. 3
   To John Dawkins 2 cyder casks   110   -.13. 9
   Ditto To 69 pint of Maloseys   -. 4. 5
   To Richard Kirklands Acct.   150   -.18. 9
   To John Gregg   30   -. 3. 9
   To Daniell Diskins for bringing a stray
     horse   -.15. -
   To James Spencer   -.19. 6
   To William Owen by agreement of Anderton   1.11. 3
   24 March 1739. Patrick Campbell presented this account which being read and allowed was OR.

Pages 220-21. Will of Richard Bullock, dated 21 Feb. 1738/9 according to the computation of the Church of England.

Richard Bullock of Prince William County.

Unto my beloved wife Susanna Bullock my whole estate both read and personal during her natural life and after her decease to be distributed as hereafter mentioned.

To my son Thomas Bullock three hundred acres of land beginning upon Skinker and Ludwell's line.

To my daughter Rachel Bullock three hundred acres adjoining to the aforesaid tract.

The rest of my land lying on the south west side of the Beaver damn to my son Richard Bullock.

To my daughter Sarah Bullock all my land on the north east side of Beaver damn.

To my son Thomas Bullock one negro man named Tom. [The above clause is contained in the original will of Richard Bullock being left out by misprision. Examined the 17 April 1752.]

To my daughter Rachel Bullock two negro men named John and Robin.

To my daughter Sarah Bullock two negroes names Harry and Toney.

To my son Richard Bullock negros Monmouth, Will and Carduo and her increase.

To my son Thomas my short gun and to my son Richard my long gun.

And at the decease of my abovesaid wife my will is that the whole personal estate be equally divided among my four children, Vizt. Thomas, Rachel, Sarah and Richard Bullock.

I constitute my two trusty and well beloved friends Charles Morgan and John Graham Mercht. to be executors of this my last will and testament.

Wit: Richard Bullock
G. Rock
Hugh Adie
Thos. Robinson

24 March 1739. Presented in Court by Charles Morgan one of the executors therein named. Proved by oaths of Thomas Robinson and Hugh Adie. two of the witnesses to it subscribed (who also swore they saw George Rock the other evidence subscribe his name as a witness).

Pages 221-22. Bond of Charles Morgan and Howson Kenner unto Denis McCarty, Gent., justice. For £ 400. 24 March 1739. Charles Morgan is exor. of Richard Bullock, dec.

Charles Morgan
Howson Kenner

Wit: Jno. Bowie
24 March 1739. Ack. and OR.

Pages 222-24. Appraisal of Valentine Barton's estate made in obedience to an order of 25 Feb. 1739.

To a servant man Edwd. Magee at   £ 2.10. -
To a servant man Richd. Millard at £ 7.10. -
Total valuation £ 79.9.6.   John Diskin
  William Addams
  Thomas ( ) Hart

1739/40   53

Appraisers sworn before Mr. Antho. Seale
Ann (A) Barton signed the inventory.
24 March 1739. John Diskin, Gent., presented this inventory and appraisment which was OR.

Page 225. Will of Elizabeth Shepherd, dated 17 Janewary 1739/40.
Elizth. Shepherd of the County of Prince William being weak in body.
Unto Elizabeth Bethun [?] and Margaret Bethun, lawfull daughters to David Bethun, all the goods contained in a Bill of sale from the said David Bethun to me not to be apriesed but equaley divided between them.
To James Nutwall my brother's son one shilling sterling.
Unto Elizth. and Margarett Bothun all my whole estate that I have left after paying my just debts and my funeral charges. I order David Bethun to see mee decently intered whom I leve my soll executor of this my last will and testament.
Wit: Elizth. (X) Shepherd
John (X) Keene
Nicho. (D) Keen
James Burk
24 March 1739. Presented in Court by David Bethun sole executor therein named. Proved by oaths of John Keene and James Burk two of the witnesses.

Pages 225-26. Bond of David Bethun and Joseph Reid unto Denis McCarty, Gent., justice. For £40. 24 March 1739. David Bethun is exor. of Elizabeth Shepherd, dec.
                                        David Bethun
                                        Joseph Reid
Wit: Jno. Bowie
24 March 1740. Ack. and OR.

Pages 226-27. Will of Nicholas Kein, dated 8 March 1740.
Nicholas Kein of Prince William County being sick in body.
Unto my loving wife Sarah Kein one half of my estate for ever.
Unto my daughter Ann Kein the other half of my estate to be paid her at the age of sixteen years and in case my daughter Ann Kein dies before she comes to the age of sixteen years then I give and bequeath all my estate to my loving wife Sarah Kein forever.
I do hereby make and appoint my loving wife Sarah Kein full and sole executrix of this my last will and testament.
Wit: Nicholas (X) Kein
William Champneys
William Burston
Mary (X) Roberts
25 March 1740. Presented in Court by Sarah Kein the Exorx. therein named. Proved by the oaths of William Champneys and Mary Roberts two of the witnesses.

Pages 227-28. Bond of Sarah Keene and William Champneys unto Denis McCarty, Gent., justice. For £100. 25 March 1740. Sarah Keene is extx. of Nicholas Keene, dec.

                                    Sarah (X) Keene
                                    Wm. Champneys
Wit: Jno. Bowie
25 March 1740. Ack. and OR.

Pages 228-30. The estate of Capt. Charles Broadwater, dec.
                                            [tobo.]   [£]
  To the settlement made by Messrs. Richard
    Osborn and James Baxter   18065   209.17. 6
  To paid William Dent his account   538
  To paid William Hale for 2 broad hoes   56
  To paid William Hale for a Judgment of
    John Withers Harpers   363   29. 9.10
  To clerks fees paid to Edward Barry   48
  To paid Mr. John West   956
  To paid Mr. Thomas Lewis for a Judgment   1497
  To clerks fees paid to Edward Barry   16
  To paid Doctor Benja. Bull his account   4.13. 3
  To paid Mr. John West in part of his estate   52. 7. 9½
  To 1 pair of Shoes pr. Charles Broadwater   -. 4. 6
  To 3 hoes had of Mr. Blackburn at 2/6   7. 6
  To 1 paid shoes at 4/6 per Chas. Broadwater   4. 6
  To paid Mr. Dulany per a lawyers fee   -.15. -
  To paid John Burk per a Judgment   -. 8. 6
  To paid to Solomon Organ   -.12. 6
  To Hugh West Admr. for his trouble and
    attendance at Stafford Court   -
  By tobacco overcharged in the settlement
    made by Messrs. Richard Osborn and
    James Baxter   80
  By Hugh West for a negro boy sold at auction
    that was taken in execution   3200
  By Mr. George Harrison for the hire of a
    negro man   786

27 Aug. 1739. Accounts settled at house of Hugh West and submitted to better judgement of the Worshipfull Court
                                    Lewis Elzey
                                    Wm. Henry Terrett
                                    John Minor
                    7 Oct. 1739
26 March 1740. Account presented in Court and OR.

Pages 231-33. Appraisement of estate of Richard Bullock, Gent., made pursuant to order of 24 March 1739/40. Appraisers first sworn before Willm. Hackney, Gent.
  Includes 8 negroes valued at £ 212.
  Total valuation £ 332.16.7½.
                                    Wm. Hackney
                                    Jno. Wright
                                    Daniel Marr
26 May 1740. Charles Morgan returned this inventory and appraisement which was OR.

Pages 233-34. An account of the estate of Nicklis Richardson, dec. [Inventory.]
  Total valuation £ 5.01.6.

1740

Jno. McKenny, administrator.
                              Tho. Willis
                              James (K) Keein
                              Richd. (R) Simson
 26 May 1740. John McKenny returned this inventory and appraisement which was OR.

Page 234. The estate of Nicholas Richardson, dec. [Account.]
1739.   [tobo.]
   To burying Eliza. Richardson   400
   Jno. (X) McKenny, admr., signed the account.
   23 June 1740. John McKenny exhibited this account which was allowed and OR.

Page 235. An inventory of part of the estate belongs to the 3 oldest daughters of Thomas Osborn, dec., named Mary, Ann and Margaret.
   25 April 1740. Signed by John Kinchelo.
   No valuation given.
   26 May 1740. John Kenchelo presented this inventory which was OR.

Page 235. Appraisement of estate of Elizth. Shephard made in obedience to an order of Court granted 24 March 1739 unto David Bethun, executor. Appraisers first sworn before Mr. William Henry Territt, Gent.
   Total valuation £ 7.19.5.
   David Bethun signed the inventory.
                              Willm. Godfrey
                              Wm. Champneys
                              John Kein
   26 May 1740. David Bethun returned this inventory and appraisement which was OR.

Page 233. A True Accot. and inventory of Wm. Sleming's estate.
   Total valuation £ 0.6.4.
   7 May 1740. The above estate of Wm. Sleming, dec., appraised by us the subscribers being appointed per order dated 25 Feb. 1739, we being sworn the date above before Wm. Payne, Gent., justice.   Thos. Lewis
                              Jno. Manley
                              John Brown

   Richard Osborn, admr.
   26 May 1740. Richard Osborn returned this inventory and appraisement which was OR.

Pages 236-37. Bond of John Brown and Richard Osborn, Gent., unto the Worshipful Justices of Prince William County. For £ 100. 26 May 1740. John Brown is guardian of Margaret Harrison, orphan.   John Brown
                              Richard Osborn

   Wit: Jno. Bowie
   26 May 1740. Ack. and OR.

Page 237. The estate of Richard Cornet. [£]. [tobo.]
1733.
1734. To pd. Mr. Thomas Pearson for rent 500
  To pd. Mr. DeLisle on accot. of a judgment obtained by him agt. the estate as per his rect. 430
1735. To pd. Do in accot. of Do as per Do 150
  To pd. Mr. Hale by accot. proved 9/6
1737. To pd. Mr. DeLisle on accot. as above as per rect. 200

26 May 1740. Richard Riccia and Elizabeth his wife, Admr. &c of Richard Cornet, dec., presented this account which was allowed and OR.

Pages 238-39. Bond of Sarah Hews and John Melton unto Denis McCarty, Gent., justice. For £100. 26 May 1740. Sarah Hews is admx. of William Hews, dec.
      Sarah Huse
      John Melton

Wit: Jno. Bowie
26 May 1740. Ack. and OR.

Pages 239-40. Bond of Esther Stone, Edward Barry and William Kirkland unto Denis McCarty, Gent., justice. For £100. 26 May 1740. Esther Stone is admx. of Francis Stone, dec.
      Esther (X) Stone
      Edwd. Barry
      William (K) Kirkland

Wit: Jno. Bowie
26 May 1740. Ack. and OR.

Pages 240-41. Appraisement of estate of Nicholas Kein, dec. Appraisers sworn before William Payne, Gent.
  Total valuation £36.2.0.
  Sarah (X) Kein signed the inventory.
      Willm. Godfrey
      Henry Boggess
      Saml. Conner

26 May 1740. Sarah Kein returned this inventory and appraisement which was OR.

Pages 241-42. Bond of Elizabeth Gaskins, Robert Hedges and Francis Searson unto Denis McCarty, Gent., justice. For £100. 26 May 1740. Elizabeth Gaskins is admx. of Thomas Gaskins, dec.
      Eliza. (X) Gaskins
      Robert Hedges
      Fras. Searson

Wit: Jno. Bowie
26 May 1740. Ack. and OR.

Page 243. The estate of Mr. Valentine Barton, dec.
            [tobo.] [£]
  To Morris Bevins [?] 3 children estate each £20.13.4   62. 0. 0
  To paid Capt. Corbet on a Judgment   620
  To pd. John Debell's accot.   0.10. 0

26 May 1740. Anne Barton, admx. &c of Valentine Barton, dec., presented this account which was allowed and OR.

Pages 243-44. Appraisement of estate of Charles Taylor, dec. made in obedience to an order of 24 March 1739. Appraisers sworn before William Hackney, Gent., justice.
No total valuation given.
23 June 1740. Mary Taylor returned this inventory and appraisement which was OR.

Pages 244-45. Appraisement of estate of William Hews, dec., made in obedience to order of 26 May 1740. Appraisers sworn before William Payne, Gent.
Total valuation ₤ 7.12.9.
       E. Washington
       John King
       Samuel Conner
Sarah Huse signed the inventory.
23 June 1740. Sarah Hews returned this inventory and appraisement which was OR.

Pages 245-46. Inventory of the estate of Francis Stone, dec.
Total valuation ₤ 26.6.2.
       Wm. Bland
       John Reeve
       George Reeve
Esther (X) Stone signed the inventory.
23 June 1740. Esther Stone returned this inventory and appraisement which was OR.

Page 247. Inventory of estate of Joseph Hampton, dec., 11 June 1749 [sic] as brought to view of Richard Wheeler, John Straughan, and John Evans.
No total valuation given.
Hester Hampton, admx., signed the inventory
23 June 1740. Hester Hampton returned this inventory and appraisement which was OR.

Pages 247-49. Pursuant to an order of the Worshipful Court of Prince William dated August 27th 1739 we have inventoried what of the estate (of Samuel McKenly who intermarried with Margaret the widow and relict of Wm. Debell deceased) was brought to our view and have set apart the orphans share of the said estate and adjusted the account of the administration.
Inventory: total valuation ₤ 18.16.8.
Account: [tobo.] [₤]
To paid Mr. Phillip Alexander for rent 630
To paid Richd. Poultney per receipt   0.11. -
To paid Wm. Hale per account proved   3.11. 7
To paid Ed. Barry per levies per receipt 241
To paid Doctr. Lawson per account proved   1. 2. 0
To paid Thomas Jennings as per account
 proved   3. 5. 2
Set apart for the orphan ₤ 7.7.7 and 105 lbs. tobacco.
       John Minor
       Wm. Henry Terrett

23 June 1740. William Henry Terrett, Gent., presented this account which was OR.

Page 249. The estate of William Debells orphans.
  1739. [tobo.]
To pd. John Sturman for balance of a lawyers
    fee by accot. proved 75
To pd. Do for Do by Do 150
To keeping him [orphan] from the 10th day of
    August 1739 to the 27th day of May 1740
    9 months and 17 days 600
23 June 1740. John Gladin exhibited this account which was OR.

Page 250. Will of David Dotson, dated 27 April 1740.
  David Dotson being sick and weak in body.
  I lend to my loving wife Amey Dotson all my Negroes during her natrel life and all my parsanel estate and if my loving wife should prove with child by me then after her decsease to the child and if the child should desease without are [heir],
  To my brother Thomas Dotson my negro man Peter
  To my brother George Dotson my negro woman Dina
  If she should have another child it must go with these young negros and all the parsanall estate [refers to Dina?]
  To my brother Greenham and Abraham and Joshua and Elisha these four brothers must draw lots for the two young negros and my parsanal estate.
  I leave my wife Ame and brother Thomas Dotson my executors.
Wit: David (X) Dotson
Robert Foster
Robert Taylor
William (W) Foster
28 July 1740. Presented in Court by Amey Dodson the executrix and Thomas Dodson the executor therein named. Proved by the oaths of the witnesses.

Pages 250-51. Bond of Thomas Dodson, Amey Dodson, William Bland and Robert Taylor unto Denis McCarty, Gent., justice. For £200. 28 July 1740. Thomas Dodson and Amey Dodson are exors. of David Dodson, dec. Thos. Dodson
                                          William (W) Bland
                                          Robert Taylor
                                          Amey (A) Dodson
Wit: Jno. Bowie
28 July 1740. Ack. and OR.

Pages 251-52. The estate of Fras. Lucas. [£] [tobo.]
  1739.
  To tobo. pd. Charles Harris for rent   250
  To cash pd. Willm. Baylis   0.12. -
  To Tobo. pd. Mr. Secretary Carter   36
  To tobo. pd. Thos. Young 115 Clarks note
      and 41 for levey   156
  To tobo. pd. Nimrod Hott   50
  To cash pd. John Gregg   0. 3. 9
  To cash pd. Richard Higgins   - 4. 6

1740   59

       To tobo. pd. Mr. Richard Blackburn   176
       To cash pd. John Carr   -.15. -
       To cash pd. Thos. Stribling   -. 3. -
       To cash pd. John Baxter   1. 4. 4½
       To cash paid Richd. Crupper   9. 6½
       28 July 1740. Anne Lucas exhibited this account which
was OR.

Pages 252-53. A true Acct. and Inventory of James Gibs Estate.
     Total valuation ₺ 6.0.1
     7 May 1740. Appraisers sworn before William Payne.
                           Richd. Osborn
                           Wm. Berkley
                           John Manley

John Brown, admr.
     28 July 1740. John Brown, admr. &c of James Gib, dec.,
returned this inventory and appraisement which was OR. And
the said admr. was ordered to deliver the estate mentioned
in this inventory together with the deced's book of accounts
to the order of the Honble. Thomas Lord Fairfax.

Pages 253-54. Appraisal of estate of Edward Young, dec., made
in obedience to order of 24 March 1739.
     Total valuation ₺ 51.1.4.
                           Antho. Seale
                           John Diskin
                           John (X) Hurst
     Mary (X) Young signed the inventory.
     29 July 1740. John Diskin, Gent., returned this inventory
and appraisement which was OR.

Pages 254-55. Estate of Mr. Val. Barton.
     1740.   [tobo.]   [₺]
       To paid Mary Ashmore   -. 2. 6
       To paid Nathl. Chapman   2.13.8 3/4
       To paid Jno. Adams   -.13. 6
       To paid Antho. Seale   67½
       To paid Mr. Jon. Horward Mercht.   1707
       To paid Jno. Young   1. -. -
       To paid Richd. Adams   -. 5. 3
       To paid Benja. Grayson   20
       To paid Jacob Remy   19. 9
       To paid Jno. Baxter   1. 1. -
       To paid Patrick Camell   14. 6
       To paid Jno. Dawkins   18. 7¼
       To paid Bond Veal   56½
       To paid Benja. Grayson   35
       To paid Jno. Diskin in Compy.   1. 6. 2
       To paid Wm. Baylis   12.11
       To paid Nimrod Hott   12. 7½
       To paid Jno. Diskin   1. 6
       To paid Edward Young   16. 3½
       To paid Mr. Gregg   12. 3
       To paid Robt. Sinkler   -. 1. -
       By Jno. Grayson   -. 3.10
       By James Grayham   2.11

By George Hays	-. 6. -
By John Owens Senr.	-. 2. -
By Thimothy Durgin	-. 6. -
By Mr. Wm. Butler	7. 6
By Robt. Muse	-.10. -
By David Dodson	-.10. -
By Jno. Hurst	4.

Dated 25 Aug. 1740.
25 Aug. 1740. Anne Barton exhibited this account which was OR.

Pages 255-57. Will of John Gosling, dated 27 March 1739.
John Gosling of Prince Wm. County in the Colony of Virginia.

To my loving wife Mary Gosling all my estate both real and personal during her natural life except she marries and if she should marry then all the estate to be took out of her hands and given as hereafter bequeathed.

To my son Simon Gosling all my lands in Prince Wm. County lying on Neabsco [?] patented by John Gosling containing two hundred acres be the same more or less, also a negroe man named Jack after the marriage or death of his mother and in case my son Simon dies before sale made of the lands or issue lawfully begotten of his body then the abovesaid lands and slave to be divided betwixt Wm. Rookard, Elizabeth Veal and Mary Colvert.

To my daughter Mary Colvert a negroe man named Ceesar to her and the heirs of her body lawfully begotten and for want of such heirs to be divided betwixt Simon Gosling, Wm. Rookard and Elizabeth Veal or their heirs to be delivered at the marriage or death of my wife.

To John Rookard son of Thomas Rookard deceased a good feather bed, sheets, pillow and cases, rug, blanket, bed cord and bed stead to be delivered him when he comes of age as also two cows and calves, two pewter dishes and 3 plates to be delivered at the same time and provided he dies before he comes of lawful age or without lawful issue then the said legacy to go to the oldest of Willm. Rookard's children when they come of age.

All the rest of my personal estate I give to be equally divided at the death or marriage of my wife betwixt Wm. Rookard, Elizabeth Veal, Simon Gosling, Mary Colvert or their heirs.

I make and appoint my loving wife Mary Gosling whole and sole executrix of this my will and Richard Blackburn and William Rookard executors in trust provided they find any waste or endeavouring to defraud any of the persons according to the intent of my will which is that my widdow may live out of it without imbezeling any part of it any further necessary for her support she then give security to my executors in trust for the same and if the legatees cannot agree about the division then my executors in trust to recommend four able persons wch. shall divide it amongst them also that no appraisment be made of my estate nor security given any further than as I have mentioned.

Wit: John (I) Gosling
Richard (R) Crupper
John (I) Champ
Charles (H) Harrison

25 Aug. 1740. Proved by the oaths of Richard Crupper and John Champe two of the witnesses.

26 Aug. 1740. Further proved by the oath of Charles Harrison. Mary Gosling sole executrix therein named being dead, on the motion of William Rookard, certificate is granted him for obtaining letters of administration.

Pages 257-58. Bond of William Rookard, John Canterbury and John Carr unto Denis McCarty, Gent., justice. For £ 200. 26 Aug. 1740. William Rookard is admr. of John Gosling.
                      William Rookard
                      John (I) Canterbury
                      John (I) Carr

Wit: Jno. Bowie
26 Aug. 1740. Ack. and OR.

Pages 258-59. The estate of John Farrow, dec.

	[£]	[tobo.]
1735.		
To tobo. paid William Dent proved Acct.		54
To tobo. paid Dr. Gustavus Brown acct. proved		574
To tobo. paid James French proved acct.		25
To tobo. paid Mr. Richard Blackburn acct.		25
To tobo. paid Mr. John Coles Mercht. proved acct.		395
To cash paid Wm. Dent proved acct.	1. 2. 6	
To cash paid Margaret Robinson proved acct.	-.11. 9	
To cash paid Majr. Champ in ballance John Farrows Bond	1. 8. 3	
To paid James Westwoods freedom dues	3.10. -	
To cash paid Mrs. Margaret Farrow proved acct.	4.10. -	
To cash paid Samuel Jackson	19.16. 2	
To my wife's thirds of the estate	66. 9. 1½	

Joseph Davis signed the account.
26 March 1740. Joseph Davis exhibited this account which was OR.

Pages 259-60. Appraisal of estate of David Dodson, dec., made in obedience to order of 28 July.
Includes 5 negroes valued at £
Total valuation £ 122.10.10.
Thos. Dodson, exor.
                      John Dawkins
                      William Addams
                      Richd. Jarvis
                      Wm. (M) Foster

22 Sept. 1740. Thomas Dodson returned this inventory and appraisement which was OR.

Pages 260-61. Bond of Thomas Duncom, Benjamin Rush and John Bush unto Denis McCarty, Gent., justice. For £ 100. 22 Sept. 1740. Thomas Duncom is admr. of John Duncom, dec.
                      Thomas (T) Duncom
                      Benja. Rush
Wit: Jno. Bowie   John Bush
22 Sept. 1740. Ack. and OR.

Pages 261-63. A true and perfect inventory of the estate of Joseph Guess, dec. 11 April 1740
   Includes 3 negroes valued at ℒ 60.10.0.
   Total valuation ℒ 167.1.7.
   Made in obedience to an order of 24 March 1739.
                               Richard Osborn
                               Wm. Payne
                               Edward (E) Vilot
   Ann (X) Guess, administratrix, signed the inventory.
   Additional inventory bringing total valuation to ℒ 168.15.3 was made 6 Sept. 1740.
                               Richard Osborn
                               Wm. Payne
   Ann (X) Guess, admx., signed the additional inventory.
   22 Sept. 1740. Ann Guess returned this inventory which was OR.

Pages 263-64. Bond of Thomas Dagg and Richard Higgins unto Denis McCarty, Gent. For ℒ 100. 24 Nov. 1740. Thomas Dagg is admr. of James Dagg, dec.
                               Thos. Dagg
                               Richd. (R) Higgins
Wit: Jno. Bowie
24 Nov. 1740. Ack. and OR.

Pages 265-66. Will of Thomas Hudnall, dated 15 Dec. 1738.
   Thomas Hudnall being sick and weak
   To my deer beloved wife Winney Hudnall her riding mare and saddle and furniture and also I give my loving wife a negro girl wch. I had with her named Susey and a bed and furniture wch. I had with my deer wife. Also I give my loving wife one large chist, one copper kettle, one iron pott and hooks and further I give to my deer loving [sic] all and every thing of wht. nature soever it be that my loving wife brought me when married that I have omited in the above gift to her for ever.
   My will is that my deer wife have the use of my negro fellow George dureing she remains my widow.
   To my son William Hudnall the negro fellow George after my said wifes decease or marry as above as also I give to my beloved son William Hudnall a negro wench named Winney and all her increese and a negro boy Jack and I also give to my deer beloved son halfe my Hoggs and halfe my Cattle and all other of my estate of what nature soever it be.
   To my deer loving wife the other halfe of my stock of Hoggs and Cattle.
   My will is that if my said son William Hudnall should dye before he come to age or have lawful issue then I give the estate to be equally divided between my three brothers and my sister or the survivor of them or their oldest child if they should leave issue.
   I give my loveing wife my wareing cloaths with what I have given her before is in lue of her write of Dower of any other parte of my estate.
   I constitute and appoint my loving brother Joseph Hudnall and my loving wife Winney Hudnall my executors.
Wit: Thos. Hudnall
Benjamin Berryman
Elizabeth French

1740/41

28 July 1740. Proved by Elizabeth French one of the witnesses thereto.
24 Nov. 1740. This will was presented in Court by Rene Napier who intermarried with Vinney Hudnall executrix therein named. On motion of said Rene certificate is granted him for obtaining letters of administration with the will annexed.

Pages 266-67. Bond of Rene Napier and Samuel Earle unto Denis McCarty, Gent., justice. For £ 500. 24 Nov. 1740. Rene Napier is admr. with will annexed of Thomas Hudnall.
           Rene Napier
           Saml. Earle
  Wit: Jno. Bowie
  24 Nov. 1740. Ack. and OR.

Page 267. Bond of John Frogg and Samuel Earle unto the Worshl. Justices of Prince William County. For £ 200. 24 Nov. 1740. John Frogg is guardian of Thomas Bullock, orphan.
           John Frogg
           Saml. Earle
  Wit: Catesby Cocke.
  24 Nov. 1740. Ack. and OR.

Pages 267-68. Bond of William Godfrey and Leonard Barker unto Denis McCarty, justice. For £ 50. 25 Nov. 1740. William Godfrey is admr. of Abraham St. Clare, dec.
           Willm. Godfrey
           Leo Barker
  Wit: Jno. Bowie
  25 Nov. 1740. Ack. and OR.

Page 269. Bond of William Simpson and Richard Simpson unto Denis McCarty, Gent., justice. For £ 100. 25 Nov. 1740. William Simpson is admr. of Thomas Simpson, dec.
           Willm. (W) Simpson
           Richard (X) Simpson
  Wit: Jno. Bowie
  25 Nov. 1740. Ack. and OR.

Page 270. Appraisal of estate of James Dagg, dec., made 17 March 1741. Appraisers sworn before Capt. Valentine Peyton. Total valuation £ 11.8.3
           Leo Barker
           Jos. Davis
           Masson Benitt
  23 March 1740. Thomas Dagg returned this inventory and appraisment which was OR.

Page 271. Inventory of remaining part of William Huse's estate.
  No total valuation given.
  Sarah Grimsley signed the inventory.
  23 March 1740. Sarah Grimsley presented this additional inventory which was OR.

Pages 271-72. Appraisal of estate of Thomas Gaskins, dec. Total valuation ₤ 48.13.3.
         Richd. Higgins
         William Farrow
         Christopher Pritchet
Elizabeth (X) Gaskins signed the inventory.
23 Nov. 1740. Richard Higgins returned this inventory and appraisment which was OR.

Pages 272-73. Will of Scarlet Hancock, undated.
 Scarlet Hancocke of Prince William County being sick and weak.
 To my loveing wife Anne Hancock the plantation where we formerly lived commonly called or known by the name of the Old Field with the land adjoyning thereto, together with four Negroes viz. Cloe, Bess, Kate and Bristoll and a third part of my stock and houshould goods dureing her natural life and after her decease the land to descend to my son John and his heirs and the negroes to be equally divided between my son and daughter John and Anne Hancocke and their heirs.
 To my loveing daughter Anne Hancocke the plantation in the forke of the Creek where William Davis now lives with all the land belonging thereto.
 To my said daughter Anne Hancocke foure Negroes viz. Titus Sharper, Sarah and Giles, and a third part of all my stock and houshold goods.
 To my loving son John Hancocke the plantation whereon I now live in the Neck on Murmnsco [?] Creek and all the land thereto belonging as alsoe four hundred acres of land left me by Richard Brett (as will appear by the said Bretts will).
 To my said son John Hancocke foure Negros viz. Nero, Galba, Poll and Jacob and a third part of all my stock and houshold goods.
 It is my will and desire that Negro Dick be sold for the most that can be gott for him.
 I ordain and appoint my loveing wife Anne Hancocke, John Gregg, Marmaduke Lawson and Moses Linton executors of this my last will and testament.
         Scarlet Hancock
Wit:
John Gregg
Ambrose (A H) Hewlet
Simon (S G) Gosling
Mary Watson
 23 March 1740. Presented in Court by Anne Hancock, John Gregg and Marmaduke Lawson three of the executors therein named (Moses Linton the other executor refusing the burthen thereof). Proved by oaths of Ambrose Hewlet, Simon Gosling and Mary Watson.

Pages 274-75. Bond of Anne Hancock, John Gregg, Marmaduke Lawson, Benjamin Grayson, Richard Blackburn and Charles Ewell unto Denis McCarty, Gent., justice. For ₤ 500. 23 March 1740. Anne Hancock, John Gregg, Marmaduke Lawson are exors. of Scarlet Hancock, dec.

1740/41

Ann Hancock
John Gregg
Mar. Lawson
Benja. Grayson
R. Blackburn
Chas. Ewell

23 March 1740. Ack. and OR.

Pages 275-85. Account of estate of George Mason, orphan.
George Mason for Disbursements on his estate in Virga.

	[tobo.]	[£]
1735.		
1736.		
Pd. Mr. Williams for schooling &c	1000	
To 2/3 of £ 12.11.6 ster. pd. Mr. Carter for Quit Rents		10. 9. 7
1737.		
Paid Mr. Williams for schooling &c	1000	
To 2/3 of 2415 lb. tobo. pd. Mr. Grant for Quit Rents 12574 acres of land	1610	
1738.		
To pd. Mr. Williams	1000	
To Mr. Jno. Mercer fees for Hall and Devin ads. Luke, Genl. Court		5. -. -
To 2/3 of £ 12.11.6 ster. pd. Mr. Jno. Grant for Quit Rents		10. 9. 7
1739.		
To pd. Mr. Williams	1000	
To 2/3 of 800 pd. Mr. Gregg for receiving rents &c	534	
To books sent for by Parson Scott		1.10. -
To Mr. John Mercer for fees Johnson		2.10. -
To Do for Cash pd. Mr. Barradal retaining fee		1. 6. -
To Do for 2/3 of fees vs. Hampton and Barrister		-.10. -
To 2/3 £ 12.1.6 sterl. pd. Mr. Jno. Grant for Quit Rents 12075 acres		10. 1. 3
1740.		
To 2/3 of 800 pd. Mr. Gregg for receiving	534	
Secretarys fees 36 Thos. Young Sherif 24 and 2/3 of 12	68	
Robt. Boggess 2/3 of 24 Clks. fees 8 and 2/3 of 178	143	
2/3 of £ 12.1.6 sterl. pd. Mr. Grant Quit Rents		10. 1. 3
To D. Bridges for schooling &c		12.10. -

George Mason for Disbursements and expences on his estate in Maryland.

1735.		
To 2/3 of 2 s. pd. Wm. Digges for Quit Rents Pr. George		-. 1. 4
1736.		
To 2/3 of 758 pd. Colo. Dent for receiving	306	
To Mr. Williams expences Annapolis		-.18. -
To Wm. Hynson for surveyors fees	591	

1737.
To 2/3 of 40 s. sterl. for Quit rents in
    Charles County pd. Mr. Brocks   1.15. 7
Pd. Mr. Simpson for half a years board   600
1738.
To 2/3 of 4 s. pd. Digges for Quit Rents   -. 2. 8
To 2/3 of 100 pd. Hammel for receiving   66
To Dr. Brown for medicines   80
To Mr. Wylie for a years schooling and books 545
1739.
To 2/3 of 4 s. pd. Digges for Quit rents   -. 2. 8
To 2/3 of 160 pd. Hammel for receiving   107
To Daniel Dulany Esqr. for retaining fee
    5 pistoles   6. 0. 0
To Edmund Jennings Esqr. for Do 2 pistoles   2. 8. -
To Mr. Savage for tending a survey at Stump
    Neck 2 pistoles   2. 8. -
1740.
To Wm. Stone Sherif for Colo. Gales fees   200
To Do for Wm. Hynson Surveyors fees   350
Account of the Crops of Tobo. of the negroes. Twelve slaves are listed.
George Mason for the profits of his estate in Virginia.
1735.
Rents received from Mr. Cocke   1060
Wm. Dent   20. -. -
John Fergerson   583
Thos. Bosman   624
Wm. Moor   524
John Bronaugh   624
Jeremiah Bronaugh   624
Jeremiah Sparks   237
Edward Violet   530
Edward Fegan   1040
Richd. Drakeford   500
Ja. Noland   220
Wm. Earp   520
Lewis Saunders   534
Peirce Noland   470
       Roocard   550
John Johnson   630
Ann Morris   1060
Thos. Gascoigne   1060
1736.
Wm. Dent   20. -. -
Thos. Yoe   730
John Ferguson   658
Thos. Bosman   624
Wm. Moor   520
John Bronaugh   624
Jeremiah Bronaugh   624
Samuel Bronaugh   624
Edwd. Violet   520
Edwd. Feagan   530
Matthew Tannahill   447
Richd. Drakeford   900
James Noland   600

1740/41

Wm. Gammerson	624
Wm. Earp	520
Lewis Saunders	520
Henry Felkins	1060
John Earp	271
Roocard	550
John Johnson	630
Ann Morris	1060
Jeremiah Sparks	530

1737.   20. -. -

Wm. Dent	
John Ferguson	630
Thos. Bosman	624
Wm. Moor	520
Jno. Bronaugh	636
Jeremiah Bronaugh	603
Samuel Bronaugh	624
Edwd. Violet	916
Edwd. Feagan	505
Matthew Tannahill	
Richd. Drakeford	700
Ja. Noland	780
Wm. Gemmerson	630
Wm. Earp	530
Walter Williams	510
Henry Filkins	430
John Earp	426
Roocard	550
John Johnson	654
Ann Morris	533

1738.   20. -. -

John Mercer	
John Ferguson	630
Thos. Bosman	624
Wm. Moor	624
John Bronaugh	624
Jer. Bronaugh	645
Saml. Bronaugh	624
Edwd. Violet	540
Edwd. Feagan	575
Matthew Tannahill	700
Richd. Drakeford	700
James Noland	285
Wm. Gammerson	624
Wm. Earp	366
Lewis Saunders	1152
Roocard	550
John Johnson	630
Ephraim Knight	900
Samuel King	530
Francis Awbrey	1060
John Gregg	2. -. -

1739.   20. -. -

John Mercer	
Wm. Hall	1470
John Ferguson	630
Thos. Bosman	624

Wm. Moor	624	
John Bronaugh	630	
Saml. Bronaugh	624	
Jeremiah Bronaugh	624	
Edwd. Violet	540	
Edwd. Feagan	550	
Matthew Tannahill	530	
Jeremiah Sparks	500	
Richd. Drakeford	849	
Henry Taylor	605	
James Noland	515	
Wm. Gommerson	624	
Wm. Earp	630	
Lewis Saunders	583	
Walter Williams	521	
John Earp	821	
Henry Filkins	1160	
Benjamin Newill	530	
Roocard	630	
John Johnson	630	
Thos. Gascoigne	715	
Ann Morris	1060	
Ephraim Knight	175	
Samuel King	530	
Anthony Hampton	601	
Matthew Tannahill for part of his rent due 1737		2.10. -
Francis Awbrey	530	

George Mason for the profits of his estate in the province of Maryland: Rents
1735.

James Sympson	586	
Jonas Parker	631	
Walter Dodson	532	
1736.		
Bayne Smallwood	1200	1. -. -
James Simpson	848	
Jonas Parker	649	
James Skinner	1068	
Moses Bell	600	
Walter Dodson	321½	
1737.		
Bayne Smallwood	582	
James Simpson	798	
Jonas Parker	583	
James Skinner	788	
Moses Bell	600	
Walter Dodson	576	
1738.		
Bayne Smallwood	615	-.10. -
James Simpson	842	
Jonas Parker	580	
James Skinner	510	
Moses Bell	600	
Walter Dodson	536	
Jeremiah Adderton	470	

1740/41   69

Contra.
1735. By Capt. Magier for a Mast   1. 1. 8
23 March 1740. Ann Mason guardian of George Mason exhibited this account to which she made oath and the same was allowed and OR.

Pages 285-86. Account of estate of Thomson Mason, orphan.
1736. To Dr. Tenant for medicines   [£] 3.18. 6
23 March 1740. Ann Mason guardian of Thomson Mason exhibited this account to which she made oath and the same was allowed and OR.

Pages 287-88. Account of estate of Mary Mason, orphan.
Includes years 1736-1740.
23 March 1740. Ann Mason guardian of Mary Mason exhibited this account to which she made oath and the same was allowed and OR.

Pages 288-90. The estate of Colo. George Mason, dec.
                                                        [tobo.]   [£]
To Stephen Lewis   534½
To Onorio Razolini 18 s. Maryland Curcy.   -.16. 2½
To Geo. Boyd £ 3.4 Do   2.17. 7¼
To Robt. Chrysty   313   1.14. 6
To Henry Filkins on Balla. of Accots.   1. 6. 8
To Mr. Cocks fees in 1736   326
               1738   30
               1740   88
To Do for Rickets fees vs. Awbrey which
   Mr. Mason was to pay   149
To Mr. Battaley for a fee Bourke   -.15. -
To Mr. Tylers fees in 1736   65
               1738   193
               1739   94
To Henry Washington Sheriffs fees Nett   27
To Mr. Turbervilles Clks. fees in 1738 Nett   144
To Thos. Youngs Sheriffs fees in 1740   36
To Mr. John Mercer for a pasty pan omitted   -.15. 7½
   for fees Summers Adm.   -.15. -
   for fees Traverse and Amees   15.
   for fees Dulany   15.
   for fees Johnson   Genl. Court   2.10. -
   for fees Brent   Do   2.10. -
   for pd. Mr. Battaley fees Fuller   7. 6
   for pd. Dr. Tenant for medicines for
      Nan Wilson [Negro slave]   2.10. -
   for pd. Barradall 59½ lb. Shorts fees
      with Noell   -. 9.11
   for fees Grigsby on Writ of error   2.10. -
   for pd. on Grigsby's execution   2053
   for pd. for Commo. receiving 1782 lb.
      tobo. and £ 10.18.8 of Staunton
      and Mounts   108   -.13. 1½
   for pd. Mr. Turberville's Clks. fees   65
   for the Sheriffs Exo. vs. West paid   20   -. -. 6
   for fees Johnson   Genl. Court   2.10. -

1740/41

```
    To Dr. Brown for medicines for Nan Wilson    600
    To Mr. Brooks 5 cows and calves £ 6.5
        3 steers                        4.10                10.15. -
    To Mr. John Mercer as pd. Mr. Barradall a
        retaining fee for fees Crupper                       -. 7. 6
    To pd. Mr. Gregg                                         -. 9. 3
    Contra.
    Balla. due Ann Mason                              49. 9. 2 3/4
    By Joseph Davis on Balla. of Accots.    930
        William Thomson                     982
        Benjamin Bullet                                      -. 5. -
        Ann Morris                          162
        Edwd. Barry                         389
        Stephen Fuller                      417
        Benjamin Cave for Mounts                         15. 1. 5½
        Cavan Dulany                                      7.10. -
        Benj. Cave for Mounts                            10.18. 8
        Leonard Barker                      276
        Scarlet Hancock                     402           4.15. 3
        John West                          448½           -.10. 6
        Mr. John Mercer as received of Sarah
            Parsons                         872
            as received of Thos. Hannton the
            balla.                         1782
        John Ferguson                       139
```

23 March 1740. Ann Mason admx. of George Mason, Gent., dec., exhibited this account to which she made oath and the same was allowed and OR.

Pages 290-96. Appraisal of estate of William Dunlap, dec. 25 May 1740.
Total valuation £ 177.15.6 3/4.
                            R. Blackburn
                            Benja. Grayson
                            William Peake

A Catalogue of Books belonging to the estate of Mr. Wm. Dunlop, deced. Total valuation £ 44.14.9.
23 March 1740. Benjamin Grayson, Gent., presented this inventory and appraisment which was OR.

Pages 296-97. Bond of William Underwood and William Hurst unto Denis McCarty, Gent., justice. For £ 20. 23 March 1740. William Underwood is admr. of Richard Price, dec.
                            William Underwood
                            William (W) Hurst

Wit: Jno. Bowie
23 March 1740. Ack. and OR.

Page 297. The estate of Mrs. Elizabeth Shephard. January 1739/40.   [tobo.]   [£]
    To John Keenes Judgement for   235   3. 7. 7
    David Bethun signed the account.
23 March 1740. David Bethun exhibited this account which was examined and allowed and OR.

1740; 1741

Pages 298-99. Appraisal of estate of John Gosling.
   No total valuation given.
   Simon Gosling, admr.
                               Leo Barker
                               Richard Cruper
                               John Kincheloe
   25 Nov. 1740. William Rookard presented this inventory and appraisment which was OR.

Page 299. Inventory of estate of Abraham St. Clare, dec., presented to view by William Godfrey, admr. Appraisers first sworn before Denis McCarty, Gent.
   Total valuation ₤ 2.10.0.
                               John Heryford
                               William Peake
                               W. Champneys
   27 April 1741. John Bowie presented this inventory and appraisment and it was OR.

Pages 299-300. Inventory of estate of John Duncom, dec.
   Total valuation ₤ 24.17.6.
                               Daniel Marr
                               William Kendal
                               Thomas Welch
   Thos. (X) Duncomb, admr., signed the inventory.
   27 April 1741. Thomas Duncum returned this inventory and appraisment and it was OR.

Pages 300-01. Will of Edward Doyle, dated 29 March 1740.
   Edward Doyle of Truro Parish in Prince William County, planter, being sick and weak in body.
   To loving son James Doyle and the heirs of his body lawfully begotten forever, the land and plantation I now live on and forty acres of land adjoyning thereto on the North side of the North run of Pohick.
   To my son Edward Doyle and the heirs of his body lawfully begotten forever eighty acres of land joyning to the land given to my son James and runing up the North Run of Pohick to my upper corner tree.
   To my daughter Elizabeth Doyle and the heirs of her body lawfully begotten for ever seventy seven acres of land the same being the remaining part of my tract, and if it so happens that she dies without heirs my will is that the same be equally divided between my two sons James and Edward.
   To my son James one three year old heifer.
   To my son Edward one three year old heifer.
   To my daughter Elizabeth one two year old heifer.
   My will is that the heifers given to my two sons may be paid them as soon as they shall attain the age of nineteen years, and that, that given to my daughter may be paid her when she attains the age of sixteen years, or after on demand.
   To my son James one sow and five piggs.
   To my son Edward one sow and five piggs.
   To my daughter Elizabeth one sow and five piggs.
   I nominate constitute and appoint my loving wife Priscilla Doyle to be my only and sole executrix of this my last will

and testament.
Wit: Edward Doyle
Simon (X) Connell
Edwd. Barry
John Connell
    27 April 1741. Presented in Court by Priscilla Doyle the executrix therein named. Proved by the oaths of Edward Barry and Simon Connell.

Pages 301-02. Bond of Priscilla Dyal, Samuel Conner and James Keene unto Denis McCarty, Gent., justice. For £100. 27 April 1741. Priscilla Dyal is extx. of Edward Dyal, dec.
                                Priscilla (P) Dyal
                                Samuel (S) Conner
                                James (K) Keene

Wit: Jno. Bowie
27 April 1741. Ack. and OR.

Page 302. Supplemental inventory of the estate of Francis Stone, dec.
    Total valuation £ -.10.6.
    Easter (X) Colvet signed the inventory.
                                George Reeve
                                John Reeve
                                William (W) Bland
    27 April 1741. Esther Colvert returned this additional inventory and it was OR.

Page 303. Appraisal of estate of Richard Price, dec., made in obedience to order of 23 March 1740.
    Total valuation £ 2.4.2.
                                George Neavill
                                Joseph Minter
                                John Neavill

    William Underwood, admr.
    25 May 1741. William Underwood returned this inventory and appraisement which was OR.

Pages 303-04. Will of Richard Drakeford, dated 13 March 1740.
    Richard Drakefoot of the Parish of Truro in the County of Prince William being infirm in body.
    To my daughter Elizabeth Drakefoot one horse called Silver, one cow and calf, a bed and furniture, two pewter dishes and six plates, one iron pot and a ewe and lamb, 2 barrows and two breeding sows.
    To my daughter Mary Drakefoot one horse or the mare called Bonny, one cow and calf, a bed and furniture, two pewter dishes, six plates, an iron pott, a ewe and lamb, 2 barrows and two breeding sows.
    Unto my beloved wife Anne Drakefoot and my sone John Drakefoot all the residue and remainder of my estate after my just debts and legacys are paid and I do hereby constitute and appoint them the said Anne and John Drakefoot to be the sole executors of this my last will and testament.
                                Richard Drakefo   [sic]

1741

Wit:
Chas. Green
John (I) Grey
Gerrard (I T) Tramol
Anne (X) Gist

    25 May 1740. Presented in Court by Anne Drakefoot the executrix therein named (John Drakefoot the executor refusing the burthen thereof). Proved by the oaths of John Grey, Gerrard Trammel and Anne Gist three of the witnesses.

Pages 504-05. Bond of Anne Drakeford, Gerrard Trammel and Michael Regan unto William Fairfax, Esqr., justice. For ₤150. 25 May 1741. Anne Drakeford is extx. of Richard Drakeford, dec.
                        Anne (T) Drakeford
                        Gerrard (I T) Trammel
                        Michael Reagan

  Wit: Jno. Bowie
  25 May 1741. Ack. and OR.

Pages 305-06. Memberdm. of the estate of Edward Droyel, dec. [Inventory.]
    Total valuation ₤ 19.6.5.
    Prasilla (A) Dioyal signed the inventory.
                        John Melton
                        William Barker
                        Thos. (T) Hicks
    25 May 1741. Priscilla Doyle returned this inventory and appraisment and it was OR.

Page 306. Will of Richard Simes, dated 8 June 1740.
    Richard Simes being sick and weake in body.
    Unto Henry Watkins Junr. one young hifer of two years old.
    My hole estate reyall and personall to my loveing wife Mary Simes hir and hir heirs for ever after my debts first paid.
    I appoint my loveing wife Mary Simes my hole and sole excetatrick of this my last will and testament.
Wit: Richard (R) Simes
Wm. (M) Watkins
Thos. Arrington
Antho. Seale
    25 May 1741. Presented in Court by Mary Simes the executrix therein named. Proved by oaths of Thomas Arrington and Anthony Seale.

Page 307. Bond of Mary Simes, Richard Jarvis and Thomas Arrington unto William Fairfax, Esqr., justice. For ₤ 100. 25 May 1741. Mary Simes is extx. of Richard Simes, dec.
                        Mary (V) Simes
                        Richd. Jarvis
                        Thos. Arrington

  Wit: Jno. Bowie
  25 May 1741. Ack. and OR.

Page 308. The estate of Richard Price. Account.
    William Underwood, admr.

25 May 1741. William Underwood exhibited this account and it was OR.

Page 308. The estate of Joseph Hampton. [£]
   To pd. Benja. Sebastian one tobo. hhd. and
     for the cost of a warrant by judgmt.
     obtained before Frans. and Jno. Awbrey, Gent. -. 5. -
   To pd. Thomas Halbert by Judgmt. obtained
     before Thos. Pearson, Gent. 7. 3
   To pd. John Straughan by Do 8. 3
   To pd. William Fearnley on execution 11. 3
   To pd. Garrard Alexander by Judgmt. obtained
     before Jno. Awbrey, Gent., 69¼ tobacco 8. 6
   To pd. Edwd. Barry 76 lb. tobacco for 2 parish
     levys 9. 6
Hester Hampton, admx.
25 May 1741. John Straughan exhibited this account which was allowed and OR.

Page 309. Appraisal of estate of Sarah Parker made in obedience to order of 24 April last. Appraisers sworn before Robert Jones, Gent.
   Total valuation £ 9.4.7.
   22 July 1738.   Leonard Barker
                              John Carr
                              William Farrow
   24 July 1738. John Chapman Purnell presented this inventory and appraisment which was OR.

Pages 309-10. Will of Samuel Bronaugh, dated 15 April 1741.
   Samuel Bronaugh of the County of Prince William and parish of Trurow being very sickley in body.
   To Susannah Allford eight hundred pounds of tobacco to be paid in three years after my decease.
   To my tow [sic] sons Francis Bronough and Thomas Bronough my piece of land containing three hundred acres lying near the great marsh of Rappahannock in the county aforesaid to them and their heirs for ever to be equally divided between them.
   To my two sons Francis Bronough and Thomas Bronough all my negros tow them and their heirs forever tow be equally divided between them as they come of age.
   All the rest of my personal estate I leave to be sold by oction and my Debts to be paid out of the money and the rest if any to my tow sons Francis and Thomas abovesaid.
   My will and desire is my estate shall not be appraised.
   I do constitute and appoint my loving father Jeremiah Bronough and my tow brothers Jeremiah Bronough and David Bronough executors of this my last will and testament.
Wit: Samuel Bronough
Jeremiah Bronough, Senr.
Jeremiah Bronough, Junr.
Jno. Bronough
   22 June 1741. Presented in Court by Jeremiah Bronough and Jeremiah Bronough, Junr., two of the exrs. therein named. Proved by the oaths of Jeremiah Bronough, Jeremiah Bronough Junr. and John Bronough the witnesses.

1741

Pages 310-11. Bond of Jeremiah Bronough, Jeremiah Bronough, Junr., Valentine Peyton and John Baxter unto William Fairfax, Esq., justice. For £ 250. 22 June 1741. Jeremiah Bronough and Jeremiah Bronough, Junr., are exors. of Samuel Bronough, dec.
         Jeremiah Bronough
         Jeremiah Bronough jr.
         Val Peyton
         John Baxter

 Wit: Wm. Henry Terrett
 22 June 1741. Ack. and OR.

Page 311. Mr. Amos Fogg and Mary Barker came before me and made oath that Guiles Easter a little before his death was in his perfect sences as they believe and that by his Desire he disposed of his Estate verbally in manner following that his whole estate of any kind whatsoever should be equally divided amongst his children.
 16 April 1741.   Amos Fogg
         Mary (M) Barker
 N.B. Guiles Easter died Monday 13th April 1741.
      Before me Richard Osborn
 22 June 1741. This nuncupative will of Giles Easter, dec., was presented by Jane his widow. Certificate is granted her for obtaining letters of administration with the will annexed.

Pages 312-13. Bond of Jane Easter and William Clifton unto William Fairfax, Esq., justice. For £ 150. 22 June 1741. Jane Easter is admx. with the nuncupative will annexed of Giles Easter, dec.   Jane (X) Easter
         William Clifton

 22 June 1741. Ack. and OR.

Pages 313-14. Bond of Elizabeth Jenkins, John Sturman and William Glading unto William Fairfax, Esq., justice. For £ 50. 22 June 1741. Elizabeth Jenkins is admx. of John Jenkins, dec.   Eliza. (X) Jenkins
         John Sturman
         Wm. (X) Glading

 22 June 1741. Ack. and OR.

Pages 314-15. Bond of Hannah Williams, Gerrard Trammel and John Murphy unto William Fairfax, Esq., justice. For £ 20. 22 June 1741. Hannah Williams is admx. of William Williams.
         Hannah (H) Williams
         Gerrard Trammel
         John (O) Murphy

 22 June 1741. Ack. and OR.

Page 315. Additional inventory of estate of Valentine Barton.
 Total valuation £ 3.18.0.
 21 March 1740. Sworn before Anthony Seal.
         John Diskin
         Willm. Addams
         Thos. (H) Art
 Ann (A) Barton signed the inventory.
 22 June 1741. This additional inventory of Valentine Barton's estate was returned by Ann Barton his widow.

Pages 315-16. The estate of Valentine Barton.
1741.   [tobo.]   [£]
To Mr. Cocke's clerks fees nett   184
To paid Robert Sinkler   0. 9. 6
To Do John Tayloe Esqr. and Compa.   2. 4. 5
To Do Mr. John Mercer   1.16. 8
To Do Mr. Willoughby Newton   0.14. 9
To Do Mr. John Graham   5. 7.10½
Cr.
By William Cornvile   0.17. 0
  22 June 1741. Ann (A) Barton, admx., signed the account.
  22 June 1741. The account of the administration of Valentine Barton's estate was presented in Court by Ann Barton his adminx.

Pages 316-17. Inventory of estate of Richard Simes.
  Made in obedience to order of 25 May 1741.
  Total valuation £ 27.18.10.
  Mary (M) Simes signed the inventory.
                        Thos. (T H) Hart
                        Thos. (T H) Hogan
                        Patrick Hamrick
  27 July 1741. Presented in Court and admitted to record.

Page 317. The estate of James Dagg, dec.
  17 March 1740/1. Account signed by Thos. Dagg.
  27 July 1741. Allowed off by the Court and admitted to record.

Pages 317-19. Inventory of the estate of Richard Drakeford, dec., made according to order of 25 May 1741.
  24 July 1741.   Richard Osborn
                            Wm. Payne
                            John Gist
  1 servant woman named Margaret Poor   £ 1. 0. 0
  1 servant man named Bryant Alliston, Taylor
    per trade   10. 0. 0
  Ann (T) Drakeford, extx., signed the inventory.
  No total valuation given.
  27 July 1741. Returned and admitted to record.

Page 319. Additional inventory and appraisment of the estate of Charles Taylor, dec. 22 July 1741.
  Total valuation £ 4.12.6.
                        George Neavill
                        John Gibson
                        Samuel Hackney
  27 July 1741. Returned and admitted to record.

Pages 319-20. Appraisal of estate of Giles Easter, dec., made in obedience to order of 22 June 1741.
  Includes one negro man at £ 30.
  Total valuation £ 79.9.0.
                        Sampson Darrell
                        John Musgrove
                        Gilbert Simpson
  First sworn before John Colvill, 25 July
  27 July 1741. Returned and adm. to record.

1741

Page 320. Appraisal of estate of William Williams, dec., made pursuant to order of 22 June 1741.
Total valuation £ 3.17.0.
        Thos. Wren
        Edwd. Ems
        Wm. Harle
27 July 1741. Returned and admitted to record.

Page 321. Inventory of John Jenkins, dec., made in obedience to order of 22 June 1741. Appraisers first sworn before Col. John Colvill
Total valuation £ 36.4.3.
Eliza. Jenkins, admx.
        David Davies
        John (I) Summers
        John Gladin
27 July 1741. Returned and admitted to record.

Page 322. Appraisal of estate of Thomas Simpson made in obedience to order of 25 Nov. 1740. Appraisers sworn before Mr. Valentine Peyton.
Total valuation £ 6.11.0.
        John Turley
        Job Carter
        Joseph Jacob
24 Aug. 1741. Returned and admitted to record.

Pages 322-23. Bond of Robert Boggess and William Payne unto the Worshipfull Justices of Prince William County. For £ 100. 24 Aug. 1741. Robert Boggess is guardian of John Smith.
        Robert Boggess
        William Payne
24 Aug. 1741. Ack. and adm. to record.

Pages 323-24. Dr. the orphans of Mr. Thomas Osborn, dec., to John Kincheloe.

1739.	[tobo.]	[£]
To cash paid Thomas Young per quit rents		2. 1. 3
To ditto paid Sarah Hogan		0.10. 0
To Ditto paid William Low		0. 4. 0
To Ditto paid Leonard Barker		0. 8.10
To paid Mr. John Graham	1002	
To paid William Foster	80	
To paid Thomas Young	40	
To paid James Fife	200	
To paid Majr. Blackburn and Young per levies	552½	
To boarding Mary Osborn from the 1st July 1739 to the 26th September 1741 at 500 per annum	1139	
To boarding Ann and Margt. Osborn from the 20th Augt. 1739 to the 26th September 1741	2100	
To tobacco paid George Reeves	160	
To cash paid Majr. Champe		6.18. 0

26 October 1741.
John Kincheloe signed the inventory.

26 Oct. 1741. John Kincheloe presented the above account of the orphans of Thomas Osborn, dec.

Pages 324-25. Estate of Charles Taylor, dec.
1739.   [£]   [tobo.]
  To paid John Bayley one barrel of corn   050
  To paid John Kemper   20
  To paid Jacob Holtclaw   2. 9. 9
  To paid John Champe   2000
  To paid Mathew Moss   0.16. 8
  To paid Richard James   0. 5. 0
  To paid Timothy Thornton   1.14. 2½
  By part of the estate sold to sundry
    persons as per bills for the same in
    hands of John Wood   19.17. 0
Ballance due the estate £ 37.7.0 and 0060 lbs. tobacco
Mary Haddocks, admx., signed the account.
25 Aug. 1741. Presented in Court by Mary Haddock, admx.

Pages 325-27. Inventory of estate of Scarlet Hancock.
  Includes 12 negores valued at £ 212.
  Total valuation £ 351.19.2.
Appraisers sworn before Valentine Peyton and Thomas Stribling, Gent.
                        Val Peyton
                        Willm. Godfrey
                        W. Champney
25 Aug. 1741. Returned and admitted to record.

Pages 327-28. Inventory of estate of Thomas Hudnall, dec., made in obedience to order of 24 Nov. 1740.
  Total valuation £ 36.14.0.
This inventory contains the statement after each entry "to my wife" or "to my child".
                        John Crump
                        John James
                        John Wilcocks
28 Sept. 1741. Returned and admitted to record.

Page 328. Estate of Thomas Hudnall
  To trouble and attendance near a month in his
    sickness   to funeral expences   £ 8. 0. 0
Ben Berryman signed the account.
28 Sept. 1741. Presented in Court by Benjamin Berryman, Gent., and admitted to record.

Pages 328-29. Will of Mary Coffer, dated 3 Jan. 1741.
  Mary Coffer of Truro Parish in the County of Prince William being sick and weak of body.
  To my son Francis Coffer all that tract of land lying in the forest of Pohick containing three hundred and seventy eight acres joyning to the land of Henry Ward on the North run of Pohick which land was entered by his father Francis Coffer before his death and hath been by me since cleared out of the office and the deed for the same made out in my said sons name.

Unto my daughter Mary More the wife of William More one shilling sterling as her full part of my estate either real or personal.

It is my will and desire that all the rest of my estate of what nature or kind soever whither real or personal may be equally divided between my two sons Thomas Withers Coffer and Francis Coffer and my daughter Ann Ferguson and I do appoint my said sons Thomas Withers and Francis my executors.

Wit:
Jno. Sturman
William Sturman
John Withers
        Mary Cofer

22 Feb. 1741. Presented in Court by Thomas Withers Cofer and Francis Cofer the exrs. therein named. Proved by the oaths of John Sturman, William Sturman and John Withers the witnesses thereto.

Pages 329-30. Bond of Thomas Withers Cofer, Francis Cofer, John Baxter and Richard Crupper unto William Fairfax, Esq., justice. For ₤ 200. 22 Feb. 1741. Thomas Withers Cofer and Francis Cofer are exors. of Mary Cofer, dec.
        Thos. Withers Coffer
        Frans. Coffer
        John Baxter
        Richd. (R) Crupper

22 Feb. 1741. Ack. and adm. to record.

Pages 331-32. Bond of William Regan, Michael Regan, Thomas Beach unto William Fairfax, Esq., justice. For ₤ 50. 22 Feb. 1741. Willm. Regan is admr. of William Regan, dec.
        Wm. (X) Regan
        Michael Regan
        Thos. (T) Beach

22 Feb. 1741. Ack. and adm. to record.

Pages 332-33. Bond of William Godfrey and Edward Barry unto the Worshipfull Justices of Prince William County. For ₤ 100. 22 Feb. 1741. William Godfrey is guardian of Margaret Bethun, orphan.
        Willm. Godfrey
        Edwd. Barry

22 Feb. 1741. Ack. and adm. to record.

Pages 334-35. Bond of Sarah Lain, James Lain and John Cannady unto Wm. Fairfax, Esq., justice. For ₤ 200. 22 March 1741. Sarah Lain is admx. of William Lain, dec.
        Sarah (S) Lain
        James (I) Lain
        John (I) Cannady

22 March 1741. Ack. and adm. to record.

Pages 336-38. Inventory of estate of Mary Coffer, dec., made pursuant to order of 22 Feb. 1741. Appraisers sworn before Valentine Peyton, Gent.
 No total valuation given.
        John Farguson
        Jeremiah Bronough
        William Peake

22 March 1741. Ret. and adm. to record.

Pages 333-34. Bond of Catherine Dunaway, Samuel Conner and Ebenezer Mors unto William Fairfax, Esq., justice. For ₤ 50. 22 Feb. 1741. Catherine Dunaway is admx. of William Steward, dec.
         Catherine Dunaway
         Samuel (X) Conner
         Ebenezer Mors
 22 Feb. 1741. Ack. and adm. to record.

Pages 338-39. Bond of Peter Rust and Nimrod Hot unto William Fairfax, Esq., justice. For ₤ 200. 22 March 1741. Peter Rust is admr. of Lodowick Jackson, dec.
         Peter Rust
         Nimrod Hot
 22 March 1741. Ack. and adm. to record.

Pages 339-40. Bond of John Gregg and John Diskin unto the Worshipfull Justices of Prince William County. For ₤ 200. 22 March 1741. John Gregg is guardian of Lettice Linton, orphan.
         John Gregg
         John Diskin
 22 March 1741. Ack. and adm. to record.

Page 340. Bond of John Frogg and Wm. Blackwell unto Worshipfull Justices of Prince William County. For ₤ 200. 22 March 1741. John Frogg is guardian of Sarah Bullock, orphan.
         John Frogg
         Wm. Blackwell
 22 March 1741. Ack. and adm. to record.

Pages 341-45. Will of Francis Awbrey, dated 14 Dec. 1741.
 Francis Awbrey of the parish of Truro and the County of Prince Williams of the Colony of Virginia being very sick and weak.
 To my loving wife all my now dwelling plantation which I now live on during her natural life, one best bed and furniture, one horse called Hurrey and furniture, three thousand weight of tobacco yearly and every year during her natural life, widowhood or day of marriage, also one negro woman called Bess and one negro boy called Cuff during her natural life, widowhood or day of marriage, likewise one servant man callen Jacob Wilson and to give to the said servant man one year of his time if deserving of it. My will and desire is that my three children may be under the care of my loving wife untill the day of her death or day of marriage that is to say Sarah, George and Samuel which is to say during her natural life or day of marriage my will and desire is that if my wife dies or marries that my daughter Sarah be under the care of my daughter Elizabeth Nowland, and my son George to the care of my son Richard Awbrey and my son Samuel to the care of his godfather Capt. Benjamin Greyson untill they be of age.
 To my son John all that tract of land he now lives upon. Likewise all that tract of land at the falls where Poutney lives upon, except fifty acres where the ferry and ordinary is kept and one hundred acres of land above Goose Creek which was bought of William Perry. Likewise all the stock and household goods which is now in his possession and call his.

1741/42

I give my son Richard that fifty acres of land reserved at the falls where the ferry and ordinary is kept, Likewise the half part of that tract of land lying upon four mile run and joining to Alexander and likewise that tract of land where Samuel Hull now lives upon extending from the beginning tree up the river one hundred yards above the ferry landing and one hundred yards above the said ferry road up to Sinkler and so joining upon Sinkler down to Clerks run.

I give my son Thomas and my son Samuel to be equally divided all the land above the land bequeathed to Richard Awbrey up to Kitocton Creek, my son Thomas to have my now dwelling plantation.

To my son Hennery the half part of that tract of land reserved upon four mile run joining to Alexander. I also give him the half part of a tract of land containing 762 acres the deed bearing date February the 12th 1739 joining to the land of Clapham and the plantation where George Williams formerly lived. The other part of that tract of land containing 762 acres I give to my son George joining upon Potomack river with the plantation, improvements, houses, outhouses where Andrew Greenhorn now lives upon.

To my daughter Elizabeth Nowland all that tract of land lying upon Tuskorora which I bought of George Hayter.

To my daughter Sarah all that tract of land where Jonathan Richardson now lives extending as farr as the three white oaks being Sinklers corner.

If it should so happen that the said Awbrey should obtain deeds or grants from the land office in Maryland for any sum or sums of land on the main or islands my will is and I equally bequeath all the said lands to my five sons them and their heirs forever they being at equal expence in clearing of the same which is to say that the money may be immediately paid down for clearing of the land in Maryland and to be equally divided between my son Thomas, Richard, Henry, George and Samuel.

To my son Thomas two of the Scotch hands namely William Frasher and John Davison, he having the liberty to seat upon any of my land during his mothers life. I likewise give him one negro boy named Jammey.

To my son Richard two negros namely old Cuffe and Mingo.

To my son Henry two negro fellows namely Jack and Nominy

To my son George one negro fellow namely Ned and his daughter Little Bess after his mother's decease or day of marriage.

To my son Samuel one negro wench called Great Bess and one negro boy called Cuff after his mothers decease or day of marriage.

To my daughter Sarah one negro girl named Winney.

I have 420 acres of land upon the branches of Cohick [sic] and 400 which I have a warrant for and have had it surveyed and expect a deed upon the branches of Clerks run joining to Richard Roberts as also another piece of land lying in Maryland over the bay purchased by the said Awbrey of Peter Froom and Elizabeth his wife for three hundred acres more or less which three several tracts I desire to be sold to the best and highest bidder and the money so raised so much as may be wanting to be applied to pay debts and the overplus the money to be laid out in negros and applied to the use of the children that is to say Richard, Henry, George, Samuel and my daughter Sarah. It is likewise my will and desire that Thomas Awbrey have fifty pounds reserved out of the price of the three tracts to buy him two negros. My will is that Thomas Awbrey settle accounts and receive with everybody in behalf of me and for his so doing for his trouble shall have full commission. My will is that all my personal estate be equally divided between my wife and six children namely Thomas, Richard, Hennery, George, Samuel and my daughter Sarah.

My will and desire is that if the above written three tracts of land when sold should not hold out to pay my debts and to let Thomas Awbrey have fifty pounds that then the money left more than will pay my debts to be equally divided between my six children that is to say Thomas, Richard, Hennery, George, Samuel and my daughter Sarah and then my son Thomas to have instead of the fifty pounds negro Butcher and negro George, except Philip Nowland pays the money to Thomas Awbrey which I have paid to clear the estate of John Neal deceased.

I ordain and appoint John Awbrey, Thomas Awbrey, Richard Awbrey to be my whole and sole executors of this my last will and testament, that is John Awbrey and Thomas Awbrey shall every six months declare upon oath in court of the increase and decrease of the estate for the satisfaction of Richard Awbrey untill he shall be of age.

Wit: Fras. Awbrey
Samuel Hull
Jas. Dickson
Jno. Wilcoxon
James (I) Mobberly
John (I) Henward [?]

    22 Feb. 1741. Proved by the oath of John Henwood one of the witnesses.

    23 March 1741. Proved by the oath of Samuel Hull and James Mobberly two of the witnesses thereto.

Pages 345-46. Bond of John Awbrey, Thomas Awbrey, Richard Awbrey, Zephaniah Wade, John Sturman, Edward Emms, John Melton, John Evans and James Robertson unto William Fairfax, Esq., justice. For £2000. 24 March 1741. John, Thomas and Richard Awbrey are exors. of Francis Awbrey, Gent., dec.

                                        J. Awbrey
                                        T. Awbrey
                                        R. Awbrey
                                        Zeph. Wade
                                        Jno. Sturman
                                        Edwd. (E) Emms
                                        John Evans
                                        James Robertson
                                        John Melton

    Wit: William Henry Terrett
    24 March 1741. Ack. and adm. to record.

Pages 346-49. The estate of Mr. Richard Bullock, dec., Dr. to Charles Morgan, executor.   [tobo.]   [£]
    To paid Thomas Acres Ayers   9. 4.10

1741/42

To paid Doctor Brown	5. 3. 0
To paid Doctor Lawson	5. 2. 0
To paid Robert Duncan	1.13. 0
To paid Martin Harden	1.16. 1½
To paid Isaac Settle	2.11. 6
To paid Jasper Billings	1. 5. 3
To paid Mary Walters	1. 8. 6
To paid Thomas Conway	0.10. 9
To paid Doctor Creig	0. 8. 9
To paid James Howard	0. 7. 6
To paid Capt. John Frogg	0. 5. 0
To paid Joseph Darnel	0. 8. 0
To paid Capt. John Allen	0. 4. 4
To paid Elizabeth Duncan	0. 3. 6
To paid John Coffee	0. 3. 0
To paid Mr. William Hackney	0. 5. 0
To paid William Coram	0. 9. 1
To paid Joseph Duncan	1.14. 0
To paid Mr. Robert Shadden for clothing for Tho. Bullock	3. 6.10½
To paid Mr. John Graham and Maj. Blackburn	12.16. 6

The orphans board and schooling

To Thomas Bullock three months	150
To Rachel Bullock seven months	87½
To Sarah Bullock one year	600
To Richard Bullock 15 months and 3 weeks	687½
To paid Mr. John Bryan for schooling	600

Cr.

By Peter Lehugh	0.10. 0
By Capt. Charles Ewel	9.19. 9
By Thomas Evans	234

Charles Morgan, executor.
24 March 1741. Returned and admitted to record.

Pages 349-50. Nichols account against Wiats estate.
1741. William Wiat and Ann Wiat Dr.

To paid Thomas Edwards for their schooling in Westmorland in the year 1734	300 lbs. tobo.

Contra.

By their proportionable parts of their father James Wiats estate as per Inventory	£ 10.12. 0
By their part of Do as per Do	120 lbs. tobo.

Signed by Wm. Nichols
22 March 1741. Ret. and adm. to record.

Page 350. Inventory of Lodowick Jackson estate.
Total valuation £ 7.1.0.
10 April 1742   Wm. Bayliss
                       Richd. (R) Cruper
                       George (G C) Colvert

A promissary note of Thomas Luis due to this estate	£ 1.15. 0
Per Ballance due per Capt. Lawrence Washington to this estate	553 lbs. tobo.

26 April 1742. Ret. and adm. to record.

Pages 351-52. Will of Thomas McDowel, dated 14 Aug. 1741.

Thomas McDowel of the Parish of True Roe in the County of Prince William, Merchant, being sick and weak in body.

I do order that in the first place the sum of two pounds four shillings and six pence be laid out by my exrs. towards funeral expenses and all my just debts be paid and sattisfyed

Unto Mary my dearly beloved wife the sum of twenty six pounds thirteen shills. and four pence good and lawfull mony of Virginia to be raisd. and levied out of my estate with all my houshold goods and my wearing apparel.

Unto my well beloved daughter Sarah the like sum of twenty six pounds thirteen shills. and four pence.

Unto my daughter Margret the sum of twenty six pounds thirteen shills. and four pence like current money.

Unto my two daughters Mary and Jean each of them the like sum of twenty six pounds thirteen shills. and four pence like current money.

Unto the child now in the womb of my dearly beloved wife please God it should live in the world the sum of twenty six pounds thirteen shills. and four pence like money. But if it please God that said child dye then I order said sum of twenty six pounds thirteen shills. and four pence to be equally distributed between the two youngest (viz) Mary and Jean.

These sums of the children not to be paid untill the children come to be of age unless that their necessity require it, and provided any of them stand in need of it that then they shall have their moiety the case appearing to these my executors.

I do hereby constitute make and ordain John Wilcoxon Senr. of Prince Georges in the Province of Maryland planter, Thomas John of Prince William County and Collony of Virginia farmer my only and sole exrs.

Wit: Thomas McDowell
John Kennedy
David (X) Griffith
Jas. Dickson

26 April 1742. Proved by the oaths of John Kennedy and James Dickson two of the witnesses thereto. The executors therein named having relinquished their executorship, on motion of Mary McDowell his widow certificate is granted her for obtaining letters of admon. with the will annexed.

Pages 353-54. Bond of Mary McDowell, John Awbrey, Wm. Halling and Francis Awbrey unto William Fairfax, Esq., justice. For £500. 26 April 1742. Mary McDowell is admx. with the will annexed of Thomas McDowell.
Mary (M) McDowell
J. Awbrey
Wm. Hallinge
Fras. Awbrey

26 April 1742. Ack. and adm. to record.

Pages 354-55. William Regan's inventory.
Total valuation £ 15.8.9.
12 March 1741.
Michl. Ashford
John (X) Sheridon
Wm. Ashford

Wm. Regan, admr.
26 April 1742. Ret. and adm. to record.

Pages 355-56. Appraisal of estate of William Steward, dec., made pursuant to order of 22 March 1741. Appraisers sworn before William Payne, Gent.
Total valuation £ 6.8.0.

W. Champney
John Kein
Thos. Moxley

Catherine Dunaway, admx.
27 April 1742. Ret. and adm. to record.

Page 356. The estate of William Steward, dec.

	[tobo.]	[£]
1739.		
To paid Thomas Conners for him	220	
1740.		
To paid Thomas Hail	1300	
1741.		
To paid John Groves	650	
To 4 hoggs of mine which he sold to Samuel Hays at 7 s. per hogg		1. 8. 0

Catherine Dunaway, admx.
27 April 1742. Examined and allowed and adm. to record.

Pages 356-57. Estate of John Queen, dec.

To paid Edward Washington 116 lbs. tobo. at 12 s. 6 per Ct.	0.14. 6
To paid Gerrard Trammel 100	0.12. 6
To paid Mark Thomas 37½	0. 4. 7
To paid John Harris 20	0. 2. 6
To paid William Hale	2. 1.10
To paid Thomas Simmonds	0.11. 6
To paid Joseph Hamilton	0. 3. 9
To paid Charles Angel	0. 6. 0
To paid John Bennit	0. 8. 8
To paid Mr. Edward Barry for quit rents	0. 4. 5
To paid Walter Williams	0. 4. 6
To paid Edwd. Washington for quit rents and 1 lawyers fee	1. 0. 5½
To paid Mr. John Brown	1.14. 6
To paid Mr. Henry Massey 600 lbs. tobacco	3.15. 0
To paid James Burn 648	4. 1. 0
To paid John Belt	0. 6. 0
To paid Mr. Edward Barry for 2 years quit rents	0. 9. 4

Signed by Elinor Pritchet, admx. of James Harbert.
27 April 1742. Examined and allowed and adm. to record.

Pages 358-59. Will of Daniel Tebbs, dated 27 Oct. 1740.
Daniel Tebbs of the County of Prince Willm. being in good health of body.
Unto my daughter Hannah Hartley one cow and calf.
Unto my daughter Margaret Atwell one cow and calf.
Unto my son Daniell Tebbs one shilling sterling.
Unto my son James Tebbs one Negroe slave named Abram.
Unto my son William Tebbs one Negroe slave named Great Jack.
Unto my son George Tebbs one Negro slave named Topsalem.
Unto my son Fushee Tebbs one Negro slave named Little Jack.

Unto my daughter Charolat Tebbs one negro woman slave named Sarah with her increase to remain in the euse of her mother Charalot till the day of her marriage.

Unto my Dearly beloved wife Charolot Tebbs two Negroe men Slaves named Jack and Abram for and during her naturall life and afterward to redound to the above named James and Willm. Tebbs.

Unto my son James Tebbs one Negroe slave named Frank after the death of his mother Charolet to be valued and appraised when at the age of fifteen years by my executors and the money to be equally divided among my following four sons James Tebbs, Will Tebbs, George Tebbs and Fushee Tebbs.

Unto my sons James and William Tebbs all this tract of land whereon I now dwell to be equally divided betwixt them, my son James to have my dwelling house at his mother Decease and that they pay yearly unto the said George and Fushee Tebbs five hundred pounds of Tobacco each yearly for four years after the said George and Fushee shall come to the age of twenty one years.

As also all my singular and my personal estate to be valued and appraised in money and that it be equally divided amongst my loveing wife Charolet Tebbs, James Tebbs, Willm. Tebbs, George Tebbs and Fushee Tebbs and my Daughter Charolet Tebbs.

I do likewise appoint and ordain my loveing friend John Diskin, my sons James and Willm. Tebbs the sole executors of this my last will and testament.

Wit: D. Tebbs
John Dawkins
Thos. Arington
Mathew (X) Mose
Thomas Attwell

28 June 1742. Presented in Court by John Diskin, Gent., and James Tebbs two of the executors therein named. Proved by the oaths of John Dawkins, Thomas Arrington and Mathew Moss three of the witnesses thereto.

Pages 360-61. Bond of John Diskin, James Tebbs, Timothy Thornton and Nimrod Hot unto William Fairfax, Esq., justice. For L 1000. 20 June 1742. John Diskin and James Tebbs are exors. of Daniel Tebbs, dec.
  John Diskin
  James Tebbs
  Timo. Thornton
  Nimrod Hot

29 June 1742. Ack. and adm. to record.

Page 361. The remaining part of the estate of Richard Sims, dec. [Additional inventory.]
  Total valuation L 3.11.6.
  19 Jan. 1741. Patrick Hamrick
  Thos. (H) Hogan

Mary (M) Sims signed the inventory.
28 June 1741. Ret. and adm. to record.

Pages 361-64. Inventory of estate of Daniel Tebbs, made in obedience to order of Court of 29 June 1742.
  Total valuation L 95.5.2 plus seven negroes valued at L 275.5.2.

1742

                        Antho. Seale
                        Wm. (W) Foster
                        Wm. Powell
John Diskin and James Tebbs, exrs.
26 July 1742. Adm. to record.

Pages 364-65. David Dodson, dec.   Estate account.
  20 Sept. 1741.   [tobo.]   [£]
  To Mary Mason for rent   545
  To George Reeves for rolling [?]   0.10. 0
  To Thomas Dodson   0. 7. 6
  Contra.
  By Mr. Ewell   0. 8. 0
  By Patrick Hamrick junr.   0. 5. 0
  Anne Dodson signed the account.
  26 July 1742. This account agt. the estate of David Dodson, dec., was presented in Court by Anne Dodson. Adm. to record.

Page 365. William Williams estate.   [tobo.]
  Paid to John Bennit in Cash   150
  26 July 1742. Presented in Court by Hannah Brewster late Hannah Williams and adm. to record.

Pages 365-66. Inventory of William Lain's estate.
  17 April 1742.
  Includes one negro woman valued at £ 15.
  Total valuation £ 79.1.5.
                        Andrew Hutchison
                        Henry Netherton
                        Vinsent Lewis
  In money paid by Colo. Henry Lee to the said Lain's estate £ 18.4.5.
  27 Sept. 1742. Returned and adm. to rec.

Pages 366-67. Bond of Sarah Ball, Ralph Hughes and Charles Morgan unto William Fairfax, Esq., justice. For £ 500.
27 Sept. 1742. Sarah Ball is admx. of Edward Ball, dec.
                      Sarah (S) Ball
                      Ralph (R H) Hughes
                      Charles Morgan
  27 Sept. 1742. Ack. and adm. to record.

Pages 367-68. Estate of Colo. George Mason, dec.
                                Md. Va.   Va.
                                tobo.   curr.
To Mr. H. Tylers clerks fees in 1739 121 109
To Mr. Cockes Clerks fees in 1739   5   4
To Mr. H. Tylers fees in 1740   40 36
To paid Mr. John Mercer for paid Colo.
  Willis's Exrs. Clks. fees   147 3/4
To Mr. Philip Keys fee agt. Minitree in
  Maryland   1. 1. 8
To paid Mr. John Mercer for paid Colo.
  Willis's executors for undercharge
  Ribban   0. 2. 8

To paid Do for paid Mr. Barradall Remr. Brents fee		1.15. 6
To Commissarys fee paid Walter Hinson in Maryland	100	
To Edmund Jennings Esqr. for Clerks fees	44	
To Daniel Dunany Esqr. for Ditto	437½	
To Dos. fee agt. Minittree		2. 3. 4
To H. Tylers Clerks fees 1740	18	
To Thomas Youngs Sheriffs fees 1739	24	
Contra.		
By Capt. William Brent	5900	
By Mr. Scarlet Hancock on account of his father		2. 5.10

27 7ber 1742. Ann Mason, admx. &c of Col. George Mason, dec., exhibited this account which was allowed.

Pages 369-73. Account of estate of George Mason, orphan, exhibited 27 Sept. 1742 by Ann Mason, guardian.

1740. George Mason for the disbursements on his estate in Virginia.

	[tobo.]	[£]
To paid Mr. Secretary Carter's fees	135	
To Sherifs fees paid Robert Boggess	20	
To Mr. Cockes Clerks fees	81	
To Robert Boggess	20	
To Mr. Cockes Clerks fees	176	

1741.

To 2/3 of 800 lb. tobacco paid Mr. Gregg for receiving	534	
To paid Mr. Francis's fee agt. Luke		2.10. 0
To paid Mr. John Mercer's fee agt. Johnson in Chancery		2.10. 0
To Priscilla Dyle for a Bond she had of his father to make over land	4000	2. 0. 0

George Mason for the disbursements in his estate in Maryland.

1741.

To Daniel Dulany Esqr. for fees Smallwood	600
To Edmund Jennings Esqr. for Ditto	179
To Hamnel for nails to line hogs heads	100

George Mason for the profits of his estate in Virga.

By Mr. John Mercer		20. 0. 0
John Farguson	630	
Thomas Bosman	1024	
William Moor	520	
John Bronough	630	
Jeremiah Bronough junr.	624	
Samuel Bronough	624	
Edward Vilet	820	
Thomas Beach	530	
Mathew Tannahill	751	
Henry Taylors son	407	
Richard Drakeford	730	
Henry Taylor	774	
James Noland	780	
Wm. Earp	400	
Lewis Saunders	522	

1742

Walter Williams	1051	
Henry Filkins	530	
Benjamin Newel	530	
William Roocard	620	0. 6. 0
John Johnson	630	
Ann Morriss	530	
Thomas Gascoigne	503	
Capt. Awbrey for himself and Samuel King	1060	
Wm. Hall	235	
Mr. Valentine Peyton	1060	

1741.
By Mr. Valentine Peyton 1060
John Farguson 630
Thomas Bosman a crop hhd. neat 1005
William Moor 520
John Bronough 630
Jeremiah Bronough junr. 624
Samuel Bronoughs exrs. 614
Edward Vilet a crop hhd. neat 842
Thomas Beach 530
Jeremiah Sparks 630
Richard Drakefords Exrs. 730
Henry Taylor 1480
James Noland 530
William Gunerson 624
William Earp 214
Lewis Saunders 350
Walter Williams 568
Henry Filkin 530
Benjamin Newel 300
William Roocard 520
John Johnson 630
Ann Morriss 530
Henry Howel 1075
Ephraim Knight 3. 7. 7¼
Capt. Awbrey's rent 530

George Mason for the profits of his estate in Maryland.

1739.
By Bayne Smallwood 522
James Simpson 1137
Jonas Parker 462
James Skiner 670
Walter Dodson 524

1740.
By Bayne Smallwood 590
James Simpson 860
Jonas Parker 602
James Skinner 570
Walter Dodson 482
By Moses Bell for rent due 1739 630

1741.
By James Simpson 964
Edward Carter 602
Edward Deveen 635

27 Sept. 1742. Ann Mason guardian to George Mason exhibited this account. Allowed and adm. to record.

Page 374. Thomson Mason. Account of his estate, 1740-42.
27 Sept. 1742. Ann Mason guardian to Thomas Mason exhibited this account.

Pages 374-75. Mary Mason. Account of her estate, 1740-42.
27 Sept. 1742. Ann Mason guardian to Mary Mason exhibited this account.

Pages 376-77. Will of Francis Wright, dated 29 March 1742.
Francis Wright of Prince William County being very sick and weak.
Unto my wel beloved wife Ann Wright her choice of half that tract of back land to settle on during her natural life and I being now apprehensive that my beloved wife is pregnant and if it should prove a boy the other half of the back land I give unto him and after his mother's decease the whole tract of land to fall to him. But in case it should prove a girl the whole property of the land to belong to my beloved wife during her natural life and afterwards to be equally divided between my three daughters if the last should prove a girl. In case any of them should die without any such heir [lawfully begotten] to the next heir at law.
My will is that my beloved wife should peaceably possess all that appertaineth unto me during her natural life except she should marry and then to possess all untill my children are of age to choose their guardians.
My will is that after my beloved wifes decease that my negros, stock and household goods be equally divided amongst my children and the heirs lawfully begotten of their bodies.
I do hereby appoint my true and trusty friends Moses Linton of Prince William County and Sigismund Massey of Stafford County executors and my beloved wife executrix of this my last will and testament during her widowhood but no longer.
Wit: Francis Wright
Jane (X) Colvert
Moses Linton
Jno. Bryan
27 Sept. 1742. Presented in Court by Ann Wright executrix. Proved by the oaths of Moses Linton and Jane Colvert, witnesses.

Pages 377-78. Bond of Ann Wright, Thomas Young and Daniel French unto William Fairfax, Esq., justice. For £ 500.
27 Sept. 1742. Ann Wright is extx. of Francis Wright, dec.
                          Ann (X) Wright
                          Thomas Young
                          Daniel French
27 Sept. 1742. Ack. and adm. to record.

Pages 378-80. Inventory of Francis Wright estate made in obedience to order of 27 Sept. 1742.
    16 Oct. 1742.   Moses Linton
                                William Davis
                                John Copher
Includes 1 white servant man valued at £ 5.0.0 and 9 negroes valued at £ 163.0.0.
Total valuation £ 219.15.4.
25 Oct. 1742. Ret. and adm. to record.

Pages 380-82. Will of Rodham Neale, dated 7 Aug. 1742.
   Rodham Neale of the County of Prince William and parish of Truro in Virginia being sick in body.
   To my beloved brother Christopher Neale my negro man named Baker and one mulatto woman named Sue to be delivered to him the last day of November next and when delivered to my said brother Christopr. to pay my beloved wife Lidia Neale ten English guineas.
   Unto my beloved brother Christopher Neale half my tract of land on difficult run.
   To my friend William Herle all my wearing apparel.
   It is my will and pleasure that my dear beloved wife Lidia Neale has the use and benefit of my plantation on difficult run and half the land to be laid of in the best manner for the use of the plantation during her natural life and after her decease to decend to my brother Christopher Neale.
   My will and pleasure is that my dear beloved wife Lidia Neale has the use and benefit of my negro man Named Apis and my negro woman Named Lucy and my Little Orfin girl named Ann Dixon and likewise I give and bequeath to my loving wife   Lidia Neale all the remainder of my estate real and personal during her natural life and after her decease the said estate given to my beloved wife Lidia Neale to be equally divided between my beloved brother Presley Neale and my beloved brother Daniel Neale and my beloved sister Francis Spencer.
   I appoint my beloved wife Lidia Neale and my beloved brother Christopher Neale to be my whole and sole executors.
Wit: Rodham Neale
Thos. Pearson
John Lucas
Wm. (H) Herle
   27 Sept. 1742. Proved by the oath of Thomas Pearson, Gent.
   25 Oct. 1742. Further proved by the oaths of John Lucas and William Herle, the other witnesses. Certificate granted Christopher Neale for obtaining probate.

Pages 382-83. Bond of Christopher Neale and Gerrard Alexander unto William Fairfax, Esq., justice. For £ 500. 25 Oct. 1742. Christopher Neale is exor. of Rodham Neale.
                              Christopher Neale
                              Gerrard Alexander
   25 Oct. 1742. Ack. and adm. to record.

Page 383. The estate of John Queen, dec. Account.
   Oct. 1742.
   Elinor Pritchet, admx.
   25 Oct. 1742. Allowed and adm. to record.

Pages 383-84. Francis Stone estate.
   1740.   [£]   [tobo.]
   To cash paid to Edward Barry   0.17. 5
   To cash paid to Charles Oneal   0.15. 0
   To Valentine Peyton   55
   To Nimrod Hot   193
   To Charles Hugget   70

```
    To Thomas Bland                             0. 9. 0
    To Benjamin Grayson                                   614
    To Mr. Brent                                          500
    To Thomas Young Sherif                                206
    To Secretary Carter                                    40
    To Richard Blackburn for levy                         152
    To Catesby Cooke  Cl.                                 150
    To Mr. Gregg for Mr. Catesby Cocke Clerks fee          24
    Contra.
    By John Kerklands debt                                200
    25 Oct. 1742. Presented in Court by Esther Colvert. Allow-
ed and adm. to record.
```

Pages 384-85. Supplemental inventory of Richard Drakeford.
    14 Dec. 1741.   Richard Osborn
                               John Gist
    No total valuation.
    22 Nov. 1742. Ret. and adm. to record.

Pages 385-86. Bond of Timothy Reading, Jasper Billing and
William Reading unto Richard Blackburn, John Grant, Samuel
Earle and Howson Kenner, Gent., Justices. For £ 300. 24 Jan.
1742. Timothy Reading is admr. of John Rector, dec.
                               Timothy Reading
                               Jasper Billing
                               Wm. (X) Reading
    Wit: P. Wagoner
    24 Jan. 1742. Ack. and OR.

Pages 387-88. Inventory of Edward Ball, dec.
    Includes four negroes valued at £ 86.
    Total valuation £ 129.18.0.
                               Jos. Blackwell
                               Wm. Blackwell
                               Jos. Hudnall
    Goods presented to our view since the first appraisment.
Total valuation [including preceding] £ 136.-.11.
                               Jos. Blackwell
                               Wm. Blackwell
                               Jos. Hudnall
    Sarah (X) Ball, admx., signed the inventory.
    28 Feb. 1742. Sarah Ball returned this inventory and
appraisement which was OR.

Pages 388-89. Inventory of estate of John Rickter, dec.
    No total valuation given.
                               John Holtzclaw
                               P H
                               H F
    Timothy Reading signed the inventory.
    28 Feb. 1742. Timothy Reading admr. returned this inventory
and appraisement which was OR.

Pages 389-90. Bond of Rose Filkins, widow, Joseph Davis and
Mason Bennett unto the Worshipful the Gent. Justices of the
County Court of Prince William. For £ 100. 28 Feb. 1742.

1742/43

Rose Filkins is admx. of Henry Filkins.
                    Rose (R) Filkins
                    Joseph Davis
                    Mason Bennitt
   28 Feb. 1742. Ack. and OR.

Pages 391-92. Bond of Mary Wallis, widow, Peter Cornwell and Charles Cornwell unto the Worshipful the Gent. Justices. For £ 50. 28 Feb. 1742. Mary Wallis is admx. of Thos. Wallis dec.
                    Mary (M) Wallis
                    Peter (P C) Cornwel
                    Charles (C C) Cornwell
   Wit: P. Wagener
   28 Feb. 1743. Ack. and OR.

Pages 392-94. Will of John Overall, dated 16 Sept. 1742.
   John Overall of the Parish of Hamilton in the County of Prince William being sick and weak of body.
   Unto my son John Overall all my land which is six hundred and thirty acres except som part that shall be hereafter mentiond. The land is in two tracts and lying on turkey run and the chestnut branch the one I bought of Leonard Helms, Ser., the other of Thomas Whitledg. The begining of both tracts is now in Whitledges mill dam and if my son John Overall should die without heir lawfully begotten of his body then the aforesd. land to be equally divided between my three daughters and also I give him two good fether beds and furniture, two negros Ceaser a boy, Judah a girl, one ovill table, one small table, on great chest, one small chest, one horse of ten pound price, sadle, pistels, holsters and sord, one cow and calf, one young stear of three year old, one sow and pigs, one ten gallon iron pot and hucks, two pot racks, one puter dish and six plates, two pistols, one iron pot off two gallons now with his grandmother, a brass morter and pestel, an iron pestel, larg a pair of tonques, a driping pan and a iron spit.
   To my daughter Mary Overall one good fether bed and furniture, one dow and calf, one sow and pigs, one puter dish, six plates, her mothers side sadle and a gelding.
   My my daughter Sarah Overall one good fether bed and furniture, one cow and calf, one sow and pigs, one puter dish, six plates, six hundred pound of tobacco to buy her a side sadle and her mothers lase hat, twelve shillings to buy her a gold ring.
   To my daughter Behethalam Overall one good fether bed and furniture, one dow and calf, one sow and pigs, one puter dish, six plates, six hundred pound of tobacco to buy her a side sadle, and a broken gold ring.
   To my son William Overall all that part of land in both tracts that is on the west side of turkey run except one acre of land that is convenient for building a mill any where on the side of the run. I give this land only for his life not to leas nor sell it but to work on it as he please himself or any belonging to him not wasting the timber and after his death to return to my son John Overall as aforesaid and also I give him one fether bed and furniture, the one hors

that is cold his and at age to act and do for himself at my death.

To my loveing mother one barrell of wheat, one barrell of corn, one hundred pound of hog meat yearly for two years this preasent year and next if please God she lives to receive it.

I allso leave my son John Overall to be with my brother Nathaniel Overall at the age of seven years to be put to school till he is fourteen and then to be cept [sic] to work till he is eighteen years old, then to be of age to act and do for himself. Allso his five negros before mentiond. to be taken with him to work for his schooling and clothing and diat and their own.

The remainder of my estate not before mentiond. to be equally divided between my three daughters before mentiond.

I appoint my good friend William Whitledge my executor of this my last will and testament and in case of his death I appoint my brother Nathaniel Overall in his steed.

Wit: John Overall
Jno. Dagg
John Whitledge
Wm. (W) Stark

  28 Feb. 1742. Proved by the oaths of John Dagg and John Whitledge two of the witnesses thereto. William Whitledge the executor therein named having relinquished his right of executorship, on the motion of Nathaniel Overall certificate is granted him for obtaining letters of administration with the will annexed.

Pages 394-95. Bond of Nathaniel Overall, John Dagg and Lewis Reno unto the Worshipful the Gentlemen Justices of the County of Prince William. For ₤500. 28 Feb. 1742. Nathaniel Overall is admr. with the will annexed of John Overall, dec.
             Nathaniel Overall
             Jno. Dagg
             Lewis Reno
 Wit: P. Wagener
 28 Feb. 1742. Ack. and OR.

Page 395. Bond of William Thorn and Thomas Harrison the younger, Gent., unto the Worshipful the gentlemen Justices. For ₤400. 28 Feb. 1742. William Thorn is guardian of John Oriar and Daniel Oriar, orphans,   William (W) Thorn
             Thos. Harrison Junr.
 Wit: P. Wagener
 28 Feb. 1742. Ack. and OR.

Pages 396-97. Account of the estate of Edward Sute.
1739.   [tobo.] [₤]
To paid William Shadburn for rolling 1 Hhd.
 Tobo.   -. 4. 0
To 3½ yds Linen made in a shift and petty coat
 for Margt. Sute   -. 5. 6
To funeral expence of ye sd. Margt. Sute 2.10. 0
To paid Benja. McColley for giting up ye
 Hogs to be apprased   -. 5. 0
To pd. Benja. McColley for gitting up ye
 Hogs to be sold   -. 5. 0

To pd. Hester McColley pr. accompt		-. 5. 0
To pd. James French pr. accompt		-. 2. 0
To ye Rent of Sutes plantation pd. Foot	530	
To pd. Joseph Exley	95	
To pd. Peter Lehew	53	
To pd. Thos. Reno	10	
To pd. John Overall as appraser	30	
To pd. William Whitledge as appraser	30	
To atta. fee pd. Batteley on acct. Sutes estate	150	
To pd. Doct. Stephens pr. acct.	1200	
To paid John Catlett	40	

1739. Crd. pr. ye sale of ye sd. Sutes Estate

By Thos. Harrison and John Gregg 24 spade sows and barros	12. 1. 0
By Do for 3 sows and pigs	1.10. 6
By Do for 4 sows and shotes	1.10. 6
By Thos. Hooper for 11 sheape	2. 0. 0
By Thos. Woodcock 1 stear	1.10. 6
By Mr. Catesby Cocke for 6 cows and calfes	7.10. 6
By Mr. John Gregg 2 stears	2. 5. 0
By Thos. Woodcock 1 sadel and furnitter	1. 2. 2
By Benja. McColley 2 Dishes and three plates	-.11. 6
By Catherin Darmont for a parcel old pewter	-. 4. 9
By John Catlett for 2 Basons	-. 6. 0
By Thomas Woodcock 2 tin pans, 1 funnel	-. 5. -
By William Whitledge 1 linen wheel	-. 9. 0
By Thos, Hooper 1 woolen wheel	-. 6. -
By John Young 1 table and Chist	-.12. 6
By Benja. Bullitt 1 pr. Handmill stones	-.13. 6
By James French 1 shot bag and gun	-.18. 6
By Thos. Woodcock for a parcel of old iron	-.14. -
By Do for 1 iron pot and huks	-. 7. 6
By Wm. Puller 2 old pots and some other old lumber	-. 9. 4
By Edw. Fegan 2 bare skins and other old lumber	-. 3. 7
By Benja. Bullet 2 beaves hides	-. 4. 1
By John Overall for looking glass and 2 muggs	-. 3. 6
By Thos. Woodcock for a parcel of old lumber	-.11. 8
By Lewis Tackit 5 old chears	-. 5. 1
By Thos. Woodcock 1 bed and furnitter	1.19. -
By Edward Fegan 1 old bed, 1 old rugg, 1 old pr. blankets	-.15. 2
By George Foot 1 old plough 2 old tubs	-. 8. 6
By Thos. Woodrock 2 fletches bacon	-.11. 6
By Wm. Whitledge 1 fletch bacon	-. 7. 6½
By Luke Cannon 1 Do	-. 7. 6
By Peter Lehew 1 gun	-.12. 1
By Richd. Tedwell	28

28 March 1743. Thos. Harrison Junr.
          Benja. Bullett   Exr.

28 March 1743. Thomas Harrison Junr. and Benjamin Bullett, Gent., Executors of Edward Sute, dec., presented this account.

Pages 398-99. Inventory of Rodham Neale made in obedience to order of 25 Oct. 1742. Made by Thos. Wren, Owin Williams and Walter English, 11 Nov.
    Includes 4 negroes valued at ₤ 109.
    Total valuation ₤ 175.14.0
    Christopr. Neale signed the inventory.
    28 March 1743. Christopher Neale presented this inventory and appraisement which was OR.

Page 400. The Estate of Charles Taylor Decsd. Dr. to John Haddox and Mary his wife Admr.

1742.	[₤]
To paid Charles Baker	1. 1. 6
To paid Peter Newport	2.16. 3
To paid Wm. Bailey	0. 5. 0
To paid Samll. Hackney	2.17. 6
To paid Capt. John Allen	2. 7. 6
[To paid John Wood	4. 3½
scratched out on original paper]	
To paid John Hitt	1. 5. 0

    Mary Haddox, admr., signed the account
    28 March 1743. Presented in Court and OR.

Pages 400-01. Inventory and appraisal of all and singular the estate of Thomas Wallis, dec. 18 March 1742/3.
    Total valuation ₤ 11.2.10.
                    George Colvert
                      Burr Harrison
                      Thomas Dowell
    Mary (M) Wallis signed the inventory.
    28 March 1743. Mary Wallis returned this inventory and appraisement.

Pages 401-02. Appraisal of estate of John Overall, dec., made in obedience to order of 28 Feb. 1742. Appraisers sworn before Thomas Harrison Junr., Gent.
    Includes a servant man ₤ 4.10.0 and servant boy ₤ 7 and two negroes valued at ₤ 45.
    Total valuation ₤ 157.17.2½.
                      Cuthbt. Harrison
                      Thos. Helm
                      John (X) McMillion
                      George Foote
                      Nathaniel Overall
    28 March 1743. Presented in Court and OR.

Pages 403-04. Bond of Elizabeth Thornberry, Thomas Stone and David Darnall unto Robert Jones, Gent., justice. For ₤ 50. 28 March 1743. Elizabeth Thornberry is admx. of Richard Thornberry.
                      Elizth. (X) Thornberry
                      Thos. (X) Stone
                      David Darnall

    Wit: Jno. Edwards.
    28 March 1743. Elizabeth Thornberry, William [sic] Stone and David Darnall ack. this bond.

Pages 404-05. Will of John Gregg, dated 14 Jan. 1742/3.

John Gregg of Prince William County being weak and sick.

To my son John Gregg all my lands above Occoquan which I bought of Mathew Gregg and Isaac Kent.

Unto my well Beloved wife Elizabeth Gregg one full third part of my Real and personall estate.

And whereas I am apprehensive that my wife if now wth. child if please God it should be a Boy and Live my will and Desire is that he shall have Nine hundred and seven acres of land two hundred and thirty six acres of said land I bought of Henry and Thos. Halley, the remainder is by Grants from the Proprietors Office to me bearing date the twenty third day of July one thousand seven hundred and forty two the one for three hundred and eighty and the other for one hundred and ninety one acres. But in case the said child should be a girl my will and desire is that she should share equally with my other two daughters.

All the rest of my lands wch. are not already bequeathed be sold at the discretion of my executors hereafter named for monney or Bills of Excha. excepting six hundred and seventy acres of land it being one moiety of a larger tract of land bought of James Morris by Majr. Richd. Blackburne and myself which said six hundred and seventy acres of land I reserve for my wife to settle on and injoy dureing her naturall life.

All the rest of my personall estate after my wifes thirds is set apart be equally divided between my daughters Jean Gregg, Mary Gregg, my son John Gregg and the child my wife now goes with.

My executors [to] make title to John Graham for one hundred acres of land and Charles Ewell for one thousand and seventy acres for which I have executed deeds.

I hereby constitute and appoint my loveing wife Elizabeth Gregg, my respected friends Benja. Grayson and Marmaduke Lawson executors of this my last will and testament.

Wit: John Gregg
John Tyler
William Smith
Andrew (X) Garner

25 April 1743. Produced in court by Elizabeth Gregg widdow Executrix therein named. Proved by oaths of John Tyler and Andrew Garner (who also make oath they saw William Smith the other witness subscribe his name).

[The original paper contains a clear impression of the seal used by John Gregg.]

Pages 406-07. Bond of Elizabeth Gregg widdow, John Grant, Bertrand Ewell, John Baxter, and William Butler, Gent., unto Robert Jones, Thomas Harrison Junr., Valentine Peyton and Howson Kenner, justices. For £1500. 25 April 1743. Elizabeth Gregg is extx. of John Gregg, Gent.

Elizabeth (X) Gregg
John Grant
Bertrand Ewell
John Baxter
Wm. Butler

25 April 1743. Ack. and OR.

Pages 407-08. Will of Marmaduke Lawson, undated.
Marmaduke Lawson being in a verry weak state of body.
Unto Elisabeth Cale all my wearing linnen, my rideing horse.
The remaining part of my estate to be equally divided between my God daughter Mary Gregg and John Handcock and I do desire Capt. Grayson may act as my executor.
Wit: Mar. Lawson
Frances (F) Peyton
Elis. (O) Cale
   25 April 1743. Presented in Court by Captain Benjamin Grayson, executor therein named. Proved by the oaths of the witnesses.

Pages 408-09. Bond of Benjamin Grayson, Lewis Elzey and Cuthbert Harrison, Gent., unto Thomas Harrison Junr., Valentine Peyton, Howson Kenner and Bertrand Ewell, Gent., justices. For ₤ 500. 25 April 1743. Benjamin Grayson is exor. of Marmaduke Lawson.
                          Benja. Grayson
                          Lewis Elzey
                          Cuthbt. Harrison
   25 April 1743. Ack. and OR.

Page 409. Bond of John Johnson and Thomas Young unto Thomas Harrison Junr., Valentine Peyton, Howson Kenner and Bertrand Ewell, Gent., justices. For ₤ 200. 25 April 1743. John Johnson is guardian of Thomas Young, orphan.
                          John (X) Johnson
                          Thos. Young
   25 April 1743. Ack. and OR.

Page 410. Inventory of the estate of Richard Thornberry, dec. 23 April 1743.
   Total valuation ₤ 15.12.1.
                          Thos. Welch
                          Thos. Jurdin
                          John Garner
   Eliz. (X) Thornberry signed the inventory.
   23 May 1743. Elizabeth Thornberry returned this inventory and appraisement.

Pages 411-12. Bond of Samuel Earle and Howson Kenner, Gent., unto Robert Jones, John Wright, John Crump and Benjamin Bullett, Gent., justices. For ₤ 150. 23 May 1743. Samuel Earle is admr. of David Williams.
                          Saml. Earle
                          Howson Kenner
   23 May 1743. Ack. and OR.

Pages 412-13. Appraisal of estate of Danl. Tebbs, dec., in Westmoreland County made by order of the Westmoreland County Court, 26 Oct. 1742.
   Total valuation ₤ 15.5.0.   John Crabb
                          George Habosn
                          John Coomber
John Diskin and James Tebbs, exors.
23 May 1743. Presented in Court and adm. to record.

Pages 413-17. Inventory of estate of John Gregg, dec., made in obedience to order of 25 April 1743. Appraisers sworn before Benjamin Grayson, Gent. 14 May 1743.
    Includes nine negroes valued at ₤ 185. [₤]
    To 1 white servant man named Andrew Garner
        2 years to serve   6. -. -
    To 1 white servant boy named Alexr. Grant   3. -. -
    Total valuation ₤ 343.-.10.
                      Val. Peyton
                      Bertrand Ewell
                      Moses Linton

23 May 1743. Ret. and OR.

Pages 417-19. Appraisal of estate of Marmaduke Lawson, dec., made in obedience to order of 25 April 1743. 18 May 1743.
    To 1 servant man named Richd. Fox 4 yrs. [₤]
        and half to serve   8. -. -
    To 1 servant boy named James Cuthull
        6 yrs to serve   6. -. -
    No total valuation given.
                      Val. Peyton
                      Bertrand Ewell
                      Moses Linton
Appraisers sworn before R. Blackburn.
23 May 1743. Presented in Court and OR.

Pages 419-20. Inventory of estate of Henry Filkins, dec. 26 March 1743.
    Total valuation ₤ 32.6.2
                      Francis Ash
                      William Davis
                      John Cooffer
Appraisers sworn before Moses Linton, 7 May 1743.
23 May 1743. Presented in court and OR.

Page 421. Inventory and appraisal of estate of David Williams, dec., made in obedience to order of 23 May 1743.
    Total valuation ₤ 13.3.8
                      Joseph Delaney
                      George (X) Henry
                      Robert (X) Duncan
Appraisers sworn before Wm. Blackwell, 22 June 1743.
27 June 1743. Ret. and OR.

Pages 421-23. Will of James French, dated 2 Nov. 1741.
    James French of Prince William County, Virginia, being sick and weak in body.
    To my son William French my Ridding horse, bridle and saddle and the best feather bed and bolster and Rugg and pair of blankets and pair of sheets belonging to me at this time and all my wearing cloaths and two cows and calves and my two hunting guns and the chest and lock and key which is called mine and one large trunk with lock and key and three gallon pewter basone and two large pewter dishes and six pewter plates and one pewter tankard, one large iron pot and one small one, two sows and piggs and all my carpenters and

coopers tools and one frying pan and one iron candlestick and a new pair of sheets and three leather bottom'd chairs and high standing bedstead and one chafeing dish and all my shooemakers tools.

To my son William French my now dwelling plantation and all the land thereunto belonging to him and his heirs lawfully begotten and in case he dies without such heirs then all that is bequeath'd to him to be sold to the highest bidder and the purchase thereof to be equally divided between my wife and all my children that shall be then living.

To my loving wife Elizabeth to live upon the plantation without molestation during her widdowhood.

All the residue of my personal estate after my debts Legacies and funerall charges are all paid I give to be equally divided between my loving wife Elizabeth and my daughter Mary Ann French.

My desire is that none of my estate be appraised nor sold and I do appoint Leonard Hornsby and John Metcalfe to be executors.

Wit: James (X) French
James Haggard
John (J) Moor
Margaret (M) Haggard

23 May 1743. Proved by the oaths of James Haggard and Margaret Haggard (who also made oath that they saw John Moor the other witness subscribe his name as an evidence thereto). Leonard Hornsby and John Metcalfe executors therein named refused the burthen of the executorship. On the motion of William French and Jarvis Ah Doggarty and their giving security certificate was granted them for obtaining letters of administration with the will annexed.

Pages 423-24. Bond of Jarvis Ah Doggarty, William French, Leonard Hornsby and John Reno unto Robert Jones, John Wright, John Crump and Benjamin Bullett, Gent., justices. For £100. 23 May 1743. Jarvis Ahdoggerty and William French are admrs. with the will annexed of James French.
        Gervas adoughhite
        William French
        Leonard Hornsby
        John Reno

23 May 1743. Ack. and OR.

Page 424. Additional inventory of the estate of Edwd. Young, dec.
  Total valuation £ 5.4.6. Antho. Seale
             John Diskin
             John (X) Husk
Mary Young, extx., signed the inventory.
25 July 1743. Ret. and OR.

Pages 424-25. Estate account of Edward Young, dec. 1740.
25 July 1743. Presented in Court by Mary Young, executrix of Edward Young, dec.

Pages 425-27. Inventory of estate of James French, dec., taken by the administrators.
         Gervase A Doughhete
         William French
 25 July 1743. Ret. and OR.

Pages 427-28. Bond of John Duncan and John Frogg, Gent., unto Robt. Jones, Thomas Harrison, Joseph Blackwell and William Blackwell, Gent., justices. For £100. 25 July 1743. John Duncan is admr. of Daniel McKenzey.
         John (X) Duncan
         John Frogg
 25 July 1743. Ack. and OR.

Pages 428-29. The heirs of Thos. Osborn, dec. Account.
1740.   [£]
To paid Capt. Berry for laying the land of 1. 1. 8
To going 5 timins on that affar to Collo.
 Farfax   3. -. -
To going 2 to Stafford Court hous to meate
 Mrs. Grant pr. Order Collo. Farfax   -.10. -
To going once to Burr Harrison Storehous by
 the same order   -. 2. 6
Cuthbt. Harrison signed the account.
26 Aug. 1743. Cuthbert Harrison exhibited this account against the heirs of Thos. Osborn, dec.

Pages 429-30. Will of Ann Morris, dated 2 May 1743.
 Ann Morris of Prince William County being very sick and weake of body.
 To my son James Leatherland one feather bed, cow and calf, two young stears, two year old and one stear four year old and hiffer and one young mare and one pewter dish and three pewter plats and one iron pot.
 All and singular my estate both real and personal household stuff and implements of household, cattle and hogs and mars and moveables whatsoever I am owner of in this world unto my son William Murphy. David Manall I give and bequeath unto my son William Murphy untill next October ensuing and then to be set free if he acquits his freedom dues for the time that he has given him which is eight months;
 I say I do make my son William Murphy my whole executor, he paying all such debts as shall justly appear due from my estate.   Ann (X) Morris
Wit:
John Daulton
Henry Howel
 22 Aug. 1743. Proved by the witnesses.

Pages 430-31. Appraisal of estate of Daniel McKenzey, dec., made pursuant to order of 25 July 1743. Appraisers sworn before Capt. John Wright, Gent.
 Total valuation £17.14.10.
         Charles Morgan
         Morgan Darnall
         Charles Morgan, jur.
 26 Sept. 1743. Ret. and OR.

Pages 431-32. Account of Jeremiah Bronaugh, Junr., as executor
of Samuel Bronaugh, dec. [£]

To paid Mr. Charles Youwell for the Bristor Company By Bond	2.18. 5
To paid Mr. William Dent by account provd.	1.18. 6
To paid Mr. Cattsbe Cock by bill	5. 2. 0½
To paid Francis Cofer for one years servis	7.13. 3
To paid Robert Linsey for his wifes servis and shumaking	4.19.10½
To three years quit rents fo three hundred acres of land	0. 7. 6
To paid Mr. John Grig by account	0.14. 0
To paid Mr. Voolintine Payton pr. account [in original paper, scratched out]	1. 0. 5
To paid William Reardin due upon book	1. 0. 6½
To paid Mosis Boots pr account provd.	0.12. 0
To paid Edward Barry By order of Joseph Rid	0. 2. 6
To paid John Bronaugh pr account provd.	0. 1.10
To paid John Martin for taking up a negro man	0.10. 0
To paid Mr. Benjamun Grason for rum and sugar for his funrall	0.16. 1
To paid Mr. Harmar Duke Lawson pr account provd.	9. 4. 7½

26 Sept. 1743. Jeremiah Bronaugh, Junr., exor. of Samuel Bronaugh, dec., exhibited this account.

Pages 432-34. Account of the estate of Mr. Wm. Linton, dec., sold at publick Oction by Benja. Grayson, John Gregg and Moses Linton, executors.

An acct. of the goods sold	to who sold [sic]	price sold for [£]
A silver tankard, a tumbler, three spoons and a pr. buckles	Moses Linton	12.18. -
A pair marking irons, a greater and driping pan	John Kein	-. 1. 6
A large chest	John Johnson	-. 9. 6
A horse skin trunk	Moses Linton	-. 7. -
A feather bed, bolster, Quilt, blanket, a pair of old sheets and suit of curtains &c	James Baxter	6.16. -
A feather bed, bolster, silk rug & a suit of curtains	Thos. Cotton	3.16. -
A diaper table cloth	Stephen Delisle	-. 7. 6
A trundle bed stead and a little trunk	Wm. Dent	-. 9. 6
2 pewter flaggons, 22 plates, 1 salt and 4 basons qt. 43 3/4 lb.	Benja. Grayson	2. -. -
7 large dishes 31 3/4 lb.	Moses Linton	1. 6. -
62½ lb. old peuter	Benja. Grayson	1.13. -
a parcell earthen ware	Ditto	-.16. -
A large bible and prayer book	Robt. Jones	-.10. -
A letter case and razor	Mr. Hancock	-. 1. 4
An old gun barrel and lock	John Gregg	-.10. -
An old looking glass and sheep shears	James Bland	-. -. 8

1743

An old broad ax, old frying pan and an old grindstone	Benja. Grayson	-. 3. 6
A whip saw and a pr. pistold and holsters	Ditto	1.14. -
An old plow and colter	Richd. Blackburn	-. 2. 8
An old copper pot and a pr. money scails	Ditto	-. 8. 3½
A warming pan	Wm. Dent	-. 7. -
2 leather chairs	John Gregg	-. 5. 6
A slate table	Thos. Monteeth	-. 7. 8
An old cubbard and Desk	John Walker	1. -. -
6 old leather chairs	John Baxter	-.13. 6
2 ovall tables	Benja. Grayson	1. 8. -
a square table	John Walker	-. 3. 2
2 feather beds, 2 boulsters and 5 pillows	Wm. Dent	4.15. -
an old trunk and a pr. holsters	Luke Cannon	-. 3. 6
2 feather beds, 2 bolsters	Mr. Ashmore	4. 5. 6
1 rug and 4 old bedsteads	John Gregg	-.16. -
a looking glass and 2 old trunks	James French	-.18. -
A large chest	Wm. Baylis	-.12. -
A candle stick and bresh	John Wise	-. 1. 8
A gun	Rodham Neale	-.19. -
One old Do	James Baxter	-.13. -
One old Do	Richd. Kirkland	-. 6. -
An old case and 9 bottles	Saml. Bronaugh	-.12. -
An old spinning wheel	Benja. Grayson	-. 3. -
One morter pestel and skellit	John Turley	-.15. -
12 old leathr. chairs and a tea table	Geo. Harrison	1.15. -
A pr. spoon molds	James French	-. 7. 6
51 lb. pot iron	Ditto	-.14. -
An old trunk	Thos. Hall	-. 4. 6
15 sheep	John Gregg	3.10. -
An old chest	Thos. Bosman	-. 3. -
49 lb. pot iron	Benja. Grayson	-.12. 6
A little trunk	Moses Linton	-. 4. -
A negro man named Harry	Nathl. Chapman	22.12. 6
An old negro man named Will and an old negro woman named Grace	John Turley	30. 2. 7

Signed by Benja. Grayson.

Pages 434-36. The estate of Mr. William Linton, dec. 1733.

	[tobo.]	[£]
To paid Mr. John Mercer a Judgmt. obtained by Pitman Scandret		14. 6. 4
To paid Denni's Conyers	500	
To paid Humphrys by proved acct.	20	
To paid Mr. Thomas Lewis by Do		-.16. 4
To paid Mr. Henry Washington by Do	499	
To paid Joseph Reid by Do	150	
To paid Abraham St. Clare	150	
To paid Alexander Clement	344	-.15. -
To paid Colo. John Colvill	594	
To paid Mr. Battaley	150	
To James French	104	
To paid John Peak	800	

To paid Ebenezer Morse		-. 5. 3
To paid Mr. Laws. Debuts	250	
To paid Mr. John Gregg	106	
To paid Ditto		3. 1. 8
To paid Mr. Thomas Hill	300	
To paid Mr. Scarlt. Hancock	832	
To paid Wm. Champneys	210	
To Doctr. James Gibb	880	
To Mrs. Ann Spore		2.12. 2½
To paid James Baxter	37	
To paid Wm. Farrow	120	
To paid Mr. John Gregg	1280	
To paid Mr. Cocke his clks. note agt. Cha. Stewart 98 lb. tobo. and 1 secretarys note 25 lb. in al Nt.	90	
To paid Mr. Catesby Cocke	1294	
1734.		
To paid Mr. Clayburne a clerks note	40	
To paid Mr. Wm. Eilbeck	74	
To paid Richd. Crooper	40	
To paid Mr. Cocke		-. 3. 8½
To paid Thomas Pinson	49	
To paid James Lovell		46.12. 1
To paid Scat. Hancock		12.14. -
To paid Mr. John Gregg	2774	
To paid Richd. Anderton by Judgmt.	557	
To pd. Wm. Dent		-.12. 6½
To paid Benja. and Jos. Tyler	1552	
1738.		
To paid Robert Jones	2222	2. 5. -
To paid Mr. Cocke Lovells Clerk's fees	215	
To paid Cavan Dulany		1. 5. -
To paid George Bret his wifes part of Fras. Linton's estate		1. 7. 1
To paid Mr. Clayburns note	28	
To paid Moses Linton his part and his Bror. John and Lettice Linton's part of Fras. Lintons osta.		4. 1. 3
To paid Fras. Jackson		46.12. 1
To paid Charles Tyler		46.12. 1
Cr.		
By recd. of Bond Veal	15	-. 2. 6
By tobo. recd. of Mr. Gregg on acct. of Washington	266	2. 4. 4
By Wm. Hall a 16 s. 8 d. per Ct.		-. 6. -
By Mr. John Gregg		-.17. 6
By tobo. recd. of Mr. French on accot. of a Judgmt. agt. Dinwiddie a 15/ per Ct.	428 is	3. 4. 3
By tobo. recd. of John Bland by Judgmt. a 15 s. per Ct.	631	4.14. 7

Signed by B. Grayson.
We whose names are underwritten have examined the accots. and vouchers. Benja. Grayson who intermarried with the executrix. 20 Sept. 1743.

R. Blackburn
Val. Peyton
Bertrand Ewell

1743/44

26 Sept. 1743. Richard Blackburn, Valentine Peyton and Bertrand Ewell, Gent., returned this account.

Page 437. Account of estate of Francis Wright, dec. [£]
```
Paid the Bristol Company at Neapsco        7. 1. 9
Paid Collo. John Tayloe, Esqr.            10. 7½
Paid Collo. Richd. Blackburn              13. 0.11
Paid Hugh Montgomerie                      0.17. 8
Paid Mrs. Grigg                            7.13. 7¼
Paid John Carr                            10. 8½
Paid Willm. Alphin                         0. 4. 0
Paid Henry Taylor                         27 lb. tobo.
Paid Capt. Cock                           80
Paid Collo. Blackburn                    123
Paid Capt. Ewell    2/6
Paid Richd. Higgins  17/ Cash
Paid Mr. John Graham Marchant             28.16. 1½
```
Signed by William Stribling
26 Sept. 1743. William Stribling exhibited this account.

Pages 437-38. Inventory of estate of John Tarph, dec., as presented to our view 26 March 1739.
Total valuation £ 4.5.0.
               John Farguson
               William Peake
               John Heryford
24 Oct. 1743. Returned by Catesby Cocke, Gent.

Pages 438-39. Bond of Susannah Smith, Christopher Pritchet and Thomas Davies unto the Worshipful Gent. Justices. For £ 100. 24 Oct. 1743. Susanna Smith is admx. of Thos. Smith, dec.
               Susanna (X) Smith
               Christopher (C P) Pritchett
               Thomas (T) Davies
24 Oct. 1743. Ack. and OR.

Pages 439-41. Bond of Bridget Fegan, Henry Berry, James Cullins, Luke Cannon and Jno. Sturman unto Robt. Jones, Val. Peyton, John Crump and Benja. Bullett, Gent., justices. For £ 1000. 27 Feb. 1743. Bridget Fegan is admx. of Edward Fegan.
               Bridget (X) Fegan
               Henry Berry
               James (X) Cullins
               Luke Cannon
27 Feb. 1743. Ack. and OR.

Pages 441-43. Bond of Charles Morgan Senr., Jasper Billing unto Robt. Jones, John Diskin, Val. Peyton and Jos. Blackwell Gent., justices. For £ 100. 27 Feb. 1743. Charles Morgan is admr. of Rosser Spicer.
               Charles Morgan
               Jasper Billing
27 Feb. 1743. Ack. and OR.

Pages 443-44. Will of Abram Farrow, dated 18 March 1741.
Abram Farrow of the parish of Hamilton and County of

Prince William, planter, being weak and infirm of body.
  My Negro named Boatswin to my son Isac Farrow.
  Negro Susan unto my beloved wife Sibell Farrow.
  Negro Sylvester unto my daughter Lidia.
  Negros Tom and Philip unto my son Abram
  Negro Goen unto my son John.
  Negro Judy unto my daughter Elizabeth.
  My will is that all my moveable estate be apriz'd and after my debts are paid that the remainder be equally devided between my daughters Sibell and Margaret Farrow.
  I appoint my wife Sibell Farrow and my brother William Farrow my whole and only executors.
Wit: Abram Farrow
John Graham
Thos. Whitledge
Daniel McClayland
  27 Feb. 1743. Presented in Court by Sibell Farrow one of the executrs. named. Proved by oaths of John Graham, Gent., and Thomas Whitledge (who also made oath that they saw Daniel McClayland the other witness subscribe the same). William Farrow one of the executrs. therein named refuseing the burthen.

Pages 444-46. Bond of Sibell Farrow widow, Thomas Harrison Junr. and Jno. Graham unto Robert Jones, Gent., justice. For ₤500. 27 Feb. 1743. Sibell Farrow is extx. of Abraham Farrow.
                                Sibill Farrow
                                Thos. Harrison Junr.
                                John Graham
    27 Feb. 1743. Ack. and OR.

Pages 446-47. In obedience to an order of Court we the Subscribers have divided the estate of James French, dec., as follows:
  Vizt. to Elizabeth French widdow of the above nam'd
  To Mary Anne French Daughter of the above Nam'd
                                John Metcalfe
                                Edward Gwatkin
    27 Feb. 1743. Ret. and OR.

Pages 447-48. Bond of Daniel Chambers, John Grant, Gent., and George Brett unto Robert Jones, Thos. Harrison Junr., Benja. Grayson and John Diskin, Gent., justices. For ₤100. 27 Feb. 1743. Daniel Chambers is admr. of Owin Grinnan, dec.
                                Daniel Chambers
                                John Grant
                                Gr. Brett
    27 Feb. 1743. Ack. and OR.

Pages 449-50. Bond of Frances Hackney, William Hackney and Daniel Marr unto Thomas Harrison Junr., Joseph Hudnall, Richard Blackburn and John Wright, Gent., justices. For ₤200. 26 March 1744. Frances Hackney is admx. of John Hackney, dec.
                                Frances (   ) Hackney
                                Wm. Hackney
                                Daniel Marr
    26 March 1744. Ack. and OR.

Pages 450-52. Inventory of the estate of Owin Grinan made in obedience to an order of 27 Feb. 1743. Appraisers sworn before John Wright, Gent.
Total valuation £ 9.9.7½.
22 March 1743.
      Daniel Marr
      James Turner
      Thomas (X) Davis
26 March 1744. Ack. and OR.

Pages 452-53. Bond of James Turner, John Garner and Vincent Garner unto Benjamin Grayson, John Wright, Joseph Blackwell and John Frogg, Gent., justices. For £ 50. 26 March 1744. James Turner is admr. of John Chilton.
      James Turner
      John Garner
      Vincent (X) Garner
26 March 1744. Ack. and OR.

Pages 454-55. Bond of Rachel Gibbins, George Harper and Samuel Jackson unto Benjamin Grayson, John Wright, Joseph Blackwell and John Frogg, Gent., justices. For £ 50. 26 March 1744. Rachell is admx. of John Gibbins, dec.
      Rachell (X) Gibbins
      Samuel Jackson
      George Harper
26 March 1744. Ack. and OR.

Pages 455-57. Inventory of estate of Abraham Farrow, dec. Appraisers sworn before Mr. Bertrand Ewell.
Includes 2 negroes valued at £ 40.0.0.
Total valuation £ 66.6.6½.
      Jno. Dagg
      Jhn, Chapman Purnell
      Simon Luttrell
26 March 1744. Ret. and OR.

Pages 457-58. Bond of Thomas Bullock and Daniel Marr unto Benjamin Grayson, John Wright, Valentine Peyton and Joseph Blackwell, Gent., justices. For £ 150. 26 March 1744. Thomas Bullock is guardian of Sarah Bullock, orphan.
      Thos. Bullock
      Daniel Marr
26 March 1744. Ack. and OR.

Pages 458-59. Will of Thomas Jordan, dated 16 Feb. 1743/4.
 Thomas Jordan of Prince William County.
 Unto John Jordans two sons Thomas Jordan and Francis Jordan one hundred and fore acres of land to be equally divided between them beginning as followeth att a corner tree of Mr. James Withers upon the ridg by Vincent Garners thence runing north to the land of Peter Newport, thence across to the line that divides me and Rice Duncan, thence along the line to the beginning to take it in neath to conclude the quantity of land herein mentioned.
 Unto my son John Jordan all the remainer part of the whole track which I am now possest with.

Unto my two daughters a track of land lying near the naked mountain containing two hundred and eighty and seven acres to be equally divided between them the eldest to have her first choice.
Unto John Royaltie a two year old heffer on mark.
Unto George Hardin a young two year old horse and all the remainder part of my estate both moveable and unmoveable within and without I leave to be sold to discharge my detts and if there is more then will discharge my debts to be equally divided amongst my children and this plantation I now live upon to be rented till my son comes of age and the rents to be for the schooling of my children.
Dannell Marr and John Duncan I do appoint my executors.
Wit: Thomas (T) Jordan
John Garner
Peter Newport

26 March 1744. Presented in Court by Daniel Marr one of the executors. Proved by the oaths of John Garner and Peter Newport witnesses thereto. Vincent Garner also made oath that he saw the testator sign seal and declare it to be his last will and testament.

Pages 460-61. Bond of Daniel Marr, John Wright and John Garner unto Thomas Harrison Junr., Benjamin Grayson, Valentine Peyton and Joseph Blackwell, Gent., justices. For ₤ 100. 26 March 1744. Daniel Marr is exor. of Thomas Jordan.
                               Daniel Marr
                               John Wright
                               John Garner
26 March 1744. Ack. and OR.

Pages 461-65. Inventory of the estate of Edward Feagan, dec., made in obedience to order of 27 Feb. 1743.   [₤]
To 1 white servant boy named William Smith   8. 0. 0
To 1 servant man named Edward Harrison   8. 0. 0
To 1 servant boy named Peter Grant   8. 0. 0
Includes 12 negroes valued at ₤ 245.
Some property at George Feagan's.
Total valuation ₤ 475.9.10¼.
                               George Neavill
                               Jeffrey (X) Johnson
                               Thos. Machen
John Diskin, justice, sworn Mr. Thos. Machen and Geo. Nevill.
Wm. Blackwell, justice, sworn Jeffrey Johnson.
26 March 1744. Ret. and OR.

Page 465. Inventory of estate of Rocer Spicer, dec., ordered made 27 Feb. 1743/4. Appraisers sworn before Capt. John Frogg, Gent.
Total valuation ₤ 8.19.11.
                               John Bradford
                               John Hopper
                               John (I) Corder
26 March 1744. Ret. and OR.

1744

Page 466-68. Inventory of estate of Thomas Jurdan, dec., ordered made 26 March 1744. Appraisers sworn before Capt. John Wright, Gent.
    Total valuation £ 40.1.11.
    3 April 1744.
                        Peter Newport
                        John Garner
                        Chas. Morgan Jur.
                        Daniel Marr
    23 April 1744. Ret. and OR.

Pages 468-70. Inventory of estate of John Hackney, dec., ordered made 26 March 1744. Appraisers sworn before Capt. John Wright.
    Total valuation £ 48.4.0.
    6 April 1744.
                        John Garner
                        Jonas (X) Williams
                        John Duncan
    23 April 1744. Ret. and OR.

Pages 470-71. Will of William Bridges, dated 31 Dec. 1743.
    William Bridges of Prince William County being sick and weak.
    To my beloved son William Bridges two third parts of my estate.
    To my beloved daughter Mary Bridges one third part of my estate.
    I constitute and appoint my beloved friend William Roe and Charles Kil [?] executors of this my last will and testament and that they may keep my children and their estates under their jurisdiction until the experation of four years from the date hereof.
Wit: William (X) Bridges
Andrew Savage (X)
Rose (X) Veale
John Lloyd
    23 April 1744. Presented in Court by William Roe. Proved by Andrew Savage and John Lloyd.

Pages 472-73. Bond of William Wroe, John Grant and Richard Foote unto Robert Jones, Gent., justice. For £ 250.
23 April 1744. William Wroe is exor. of William Bridges.
                        Wm. Wroe
                        John Grant
                        Richard Foote

Pages 473-74. Will of Jonas Williams, Jr., dated 30 Jan. 1743/4.
    Jonas Williams, Junr., of Prince William County being sick and weak.
    To my beloved son David Williams one hundred and eleven acres of land joining to the land of John Wright, Gent., and the land of Simon Morgan.
    To my beloved son Jonas Williams one hundred and sixteen acres of land being the lot that Jacob Darnall now lives on.
    To my beloved son James Williams one hundred and thirty three acres of land joining to the land of Doctor Bell deceased.

Unto the use of my well beloved wife Ann Williams all my moveable estate during her widowhood or natural life and if she marries to be equally divided among my three sons before named.
    I constitute and appoint my well beloved wife Ann Williams executrix and my beloved friend John Wright, Gent., executor of this my last will and testament.
Wit: Jonas Williams
Vincent (X) Garner
John Lloyd
Elizabeth (X) Sinclair
    23 April 1744. Presented in Court by Ann Williams one of the executors therein named. Proved by the oaths of Vincent Garner and John Lloyd.

Pages 475-76. Bond of Ann Williams, John Ambrose and Augustine Finnings [Jennings] unto Robert Jones, Gent., justice. For £250. 23 April 1744. Ann Williams is extx. of Jonas Williams Junr., dec.   Ann (X) Williams
                                        John Ambrose
                                        Augustine Jennings

    23 April 1744. Ack. and OR.

Pages 476-77. Will of Thomas Deakers, dated 10 Feb. 1743/4.
    Thomas Deakers of Prince William County being sick and weak.
    To my beloved friend John Wright one orphan boy named John Edwards to serve his indentured time and all my moveable estate (except one bed and one cow).
    To Margaret Morgan one cow.
    To Morgan Darnall the bed whereon I now lyeth upon in requital of all I have ever received from him.
    I do appoint my beloved friend John Ambrose executor of this my last will and testament.
Wit: Thomas (T D) Deakers
John Wright
John Lloyd
    23 April 1744. Presented in Court by John Ambrose executor therein named. Proved by all the witnesses thereto.

Pages 477-78. Bond of John Ambrose and Samuel Earle unto Robert Jones, Gent., justice. For £50. 23 April 1744. John Ambrose is exor. of Thomas Deakers.
                                        John Ambrose
                                        Sam Earle
    23 April 1744. Ack. and OR.

Pages 478-80. Bond of Sarah Kendall, Morgan Darnal and Thomas Kendall unto Thomas Harrison Junr., Richard Blackburn, John Wright and William Blackwell, Gent., justices. For £100. 23 April 1744. Sarah Kendall is admx. of William Kendall, dec.
                                        Sarah Kendal
                                        Thos. (X) Kendal
                                        Morgan (M D) Darnall
    23 April 1744. Ack. and OR.

Page 430. Inventory of estate of Thomas Smith.
  Total valuation ₤ 17.4.10½.
  26 Nov. 1743.   Robert Hedges
                               Henry Howdl
                               John Cotten
  23 April 1744. Ret. and OR.

Page 431. Estate of Thomas Smith, dec., to Susanna Smith.
Nov. 1743.
  Account signed by Susa. Smith
  23 April 1744. Presented in Court by Susanna Smith.

Pages 481-82. Inventory of estate of John Chelton, dec., ordered made 26 March 1744. Appraisers sworn before Capt. John Frogg, Gent.
  Total valuation ₤ 12.7.0.
  31 March 1744.   Thomas Grimsley
                               James Fletcher
                               John Fletcher
  23 April 1744. Ret. and OR.

Pages 482-83. Will of John Marr, dated 8 May 1744.
  John Marr of New Hamilton Parish and County of Prince William being very sick and weak in body.
  To Elizabeth Marr my beloved wife, my negro boy Peter and my orphan boy James Sims at her own disposeal and the third part of my estate beside as household goods and creatures, corn, wheat and rie and tobacco and my estate not to be sold till she hath her thirds but to divided by three honest men such as the Court shall appoint.
  To John Bradford, Junr., my negro boy Tom after my decease and the said Bradford shall oblige himself to pay to Martha Keirns five pounds Currt. mony in the space of one year.
  To John Marr the son of Daniel Marr my negro girl Cate after my decease. And the said Marr shall oblige himself to pay Mary Nettle six pounds currt. money at the age of eighteen.
  To my beloved son Christopher Marr my servt. woman Isbel Sims.
  To John Rector my young grey mare Pug, bridle and saddle and her increase, and the remainder part of my estate to be equally divided amongst my children.
  I do appoint Daniel Marr and John Bradford executors of this my last will and testament.
Wit: John Marr
Stephen (S) Smith
William (X) Sparks
James (X) Stephenson
  28 May 1744. Presented in Court by Daniel Marr and John Bradford executors therein named. Proved by all the witnesses.

Pages 484-85. Bond of Daniel Marr, John Bradford, Joseph Hudnall and William Blackwell unto Robert Jones, Gent., justice. For ₤ 400. 28 May 1744. Daniel Marr and John Bradford are exors. of John Marr.

                                    Daniel Marr
                                    John (X) Bradford
                                    Jos. Hudnall
                                    Wm. Blackwell
29 May 1744. Ack. and OR.

Pages 485-87. Will of John Page, dated 10 Nov. 1743 according to the computation of the Church of England.
John Page of Prince William County.
To my son William Page one young mare saddle and bridle and one gun with all my body of cloaths and to be free to act and do for himself at the age of eighteen years.
To my beloved wife Elizabeth Page the remaining part of my estate both real and personal (that is to say) the use and benefit of the same towards the maintainence of her self and my children during her widohood or natural life and dureing the said time I constitute and appoint my abovesd. wife to be whole and sole executres and also a garden to my children and no securyty to be given and after the day of her marriage or decease I constitute nominate and appoint my true trusty and well beloved friend Charles Morgan to be my whole and sole executor whom also I do hereby inpower and authororise to sell and dispose of at publick oction all my lands and negroes for the best price that can be got in cash and the same to equily divided among my daughters as they come to the age of sixteen years at which age my desire is that they may all be set at liberty to act and do for themselves and as to my personal estate my desire is that it be kept in spacie and also equily divided among my daughters as they come of age (Vizt) Hanah, Elizabeth, Grace, Sarah, and the child that my wife now goes with.
I also appoint my trusty and beloved friend Charles Morgan to be garden to my said children after the decease of my wife.
                                                John Page
I desire that my within mentioned estate be neither appraised nor sold during my wife's widdowhood or natural life.
Wit: John Page
John Edwards
Stephen (X) Lathem
Daniel Bradford
28 May 1744. Presented in Court by Elizabeth Page, widow, executrix therein named. Proved by all the witnesses.

Pages 487-88. Will of Francis Lacon, dated 30 April 1744.
Francis Lacon of the County of Prince William in Virginia being very sick and weak in body.
To Rachel Spiller wife of William Spiller Junr. two negro boys one named Joseph, the other, Jemmy, to be delivered to her after the death of my wife, not that her husband shall have anything to do with them or to have any command over them nor any person or persons whatsoever but only to whom she shall dispose of them too.
To my well beloved wife Jane Lacon three negros that is one negro woman called Pegg, one negro guirl named Pender and one negro boy named Ben with all other my personal estate of what nature kind or quality soever.

I do hereby constitute my beloved Jane Lacon my sole executrix of this my last will and testament desiring the said Rachel Spiller to be assis to her.
Wit: Francis Lacon
Wm. Tackett
Katherine (X) Waters
Sarah (X) Taquett
    28 May 1744. Presented in Court by Jane Lacon widow, executrix therein named. Proved by all the witnesses.

Pages 489-90. Bond of Jane Lacon, Edward Gwatkin and John Tackett unto Robert Jones, Gent., justice. For £ 500. 28 May 1744. Jane Lacon is extx. of Francis Lacon, dec.
                             Jane (X) Lacon
                             Edward Gwatkin
                             John Tackett
    28 May 1744. Ack. and OR.

Pages 490-91. Will of Simon Gosling, dated 23 Oct. 1743.
    Simon Gosling of the County of Prince William being very sick and weak of body.
    Unto my brother William Rookard and to his heirs forever my horse called Beaver and also if my said brother shall think proper to give up the lease unto my loving wife for the plantation where he now lives, I give unto him, his heirs or assigns the sum of five pounds current money of Virginia.
    To my dear wife Jane one half of my whole estate both real and personal.
    To my child that my dear wife now travels with the other half of my estate. It is my will and desire if my said child die without heirs that the estate left it should go to my brother William Rookards children now born and their heirs.
    It is my will and desire that my said child my dear wife is now big with have its estate when it shall attain to the age of eighteen years and till then to remain in the hands of my executors.
    I do appoint my dear wife and my loving brother William Rookard whole executors of this my last will and testament.
Wit: Simon (X) Gosling
Bertrand Ewell
Charles Tyler
Wm. Ridley
    28 May 1744. Presented in Court by Jane Gosling, widow, executrix therein named. Proved by all the witnesses.

Pages 491-93. Bond of Jane Gosling, John Cantaberry and Andrew Dalton unto Thomas Harrison, Richard Blackburn, William Blackwell and William Butler, Gent., justices. For £ 500. 28 May 1744. Jane Gosling is extx. of Simon Gosling.
                           Jane (X) Gosling
                           Andrew Dalton
                           John (I) Cantaberry
    28 May 1744. Ack. and OR.

Pages 493-94. Bond of William Hancock, Moses Linton and Bertrand Ewell unto Thomas Harrison, Richard Blackburn,

William Blackwell and John Crump, Gent., justices. For L 1200. 28 May 1744. William Hancock is guardian of George Hancock, orphan.
                                William Hancock
                                Bertrand Ewell
                                Moses Linton

   28 May 1744. Ack. and OR.

Pages 494-95. Inventory of estate of Thomas Dacon [Deaker] made in obedience to order of 23 April 1744. Appraisers sworn before John Wright, Gent.
   Includes one servant boy valued at L 12.0.0.
   Total valuation L 22.13.9.
                                Jonas (I) Williams
                                John Darnall
                                Thomas Stone

   28 May 1744. Ret. and OR.

Pages 495-96. Inventory of estate of William Kendall, dec., ordered made 23 April 1744. Appraisers sworn before Capt. John Wright, Gent.
   Total valuation L 20.9.10.
   1 May 1744.
                                John Garner
                                James Fletcher
                                Peter Newport

   28 May 1744. Ret. and OR.

Pages 496-97. Inventory of estate of John Gibbons, made in obedience to order of 26 March 1744.
   Total valuation L 5.4.6.
                                John Kincheloe
                                Thos. Jones
                                Samll. Harper

   25 June 1744. Ret. and OR.

Pages 497-98. Inventory of estate of Jonas Williams, Junr., ordered made 23 April [1744]. Appraisers sworn before Capt. John Wright, Gent.
   Includes one servant woman valued at L 7 and one negro man valued at L 35.
   Total valuation L 84.6.2.
   22 May 1744.
                                Charles Morgan
                                Daniel Marr
                                John Garner

   25 June 1744. Ret. and OR.

Pages 498-503. Inventory of estate of John Marr, made in obedience to order of 28 May 1744. Appraisers sworn before John Wright.
   Includes 3 negroes valued at L 79.10.0, one servant man valued at L 6.10.0, one servant woman valued at L 7, and one orphan boy valued at L 5.
   No total valuation given.
                                John Grant
                                Jos. Hudnall
                                Jacob Holtzclaw

   25 June 1744. Ret. and OR.

Pages 503-04. Additional inventory of the estate of Abra.
Farrow. [L]
  Includes 2 negroes valued at L 40.
  To 1 old decreped servant man four years to
    serve, one half belonging to the estate
    at 40/   1. -. -
  Total valuation L 41.5.0.
          Simon Luttrell
          John Chapman Purnall
          John Dagg
  25 June 1744. Ret. and OR.

Pages 504-05. Additional inventory of estate of Edward Feagin, dec., taken 11 June 1744. Appraisers sworn before John Diskin, Gent.
  Includes two negroes.
  Total valuation L 29.1.8.
          George Neavill
          Jeoffry (X) Johnson
          Thos. Machen
  Bridget Feagin, admx.
  25 June 1744. Ret. and OR.

Pages 505-06. Will of James Greshon, dated 23 Feb. 1743/4.
  James Greshon of Prince William County being sick and weak.
  To my beloved daughter Mary Greshon and my beloved daughter Elizabeth Morris my whole estate to be equally divided between them.
  I constitute and appoint my beloved son in law Thomas Morris executor and my beloved daughter Mary Greshon executrix of this my last will and testament.
Wit: James (I) Greshon
James Fletcher
Thomas Grimsley
John Lloyd
  25 June 1744. Presented in Court by Thos. Morris and Mary Greshon executors therein named. Proved by the oaths of James Fletcher and Thomas Grimsley, two of the witnesses.

Pages 507-08. Bond of Thos. Morris, Mary Greshon, William Hackney and James Fletcher unto Thomas Harrison Junr., Richard Blackburn, John Wright and William Blackwell, Gent., justices. For L 200. 25 June 1744. Thomas and Mary are exors. of James Greshon.   Thos. (X) Morris
          Mary Greecion
          Wm. Hackney
          James Fletcher
  28 June 1744. Ack. and OR.

Pages 508-09. Bond of Edward Feagan, Daniel Feagin, Henry Feagan unto Thomas Harrison Junr., Richard Blackburn, John Wright and Joseph Blackwell, Gent., justices. For L 300. 26 June 1744. Edward is guardian of Francis Feagan, orphan.
          Edward Feagan
          Daniel Feagin
          Henry Feagin
  28 June 1744. Ack. and OR.

Pages 509-11. Bond of Elizabeth Bailey, John Haddox and William
Wyatt unto Benjamin Grayson, John Wright, Val. Peyton and Moses
Linton, Gent., justices. For ₤ 50. 23 July 1744. Elizabeth
Bailey is admx. of John White, dec.
         Elizabeth (E) Bailey
         John (I) Haddox
         William Wyatt
 23 July 1744. Ack. and OR.

Pages 511-12. Bond of George Byrn and Cuthbert Harrison, Gent.,
unto Robert Jones, Richard Blackburn, Benjamin Grayson and
John Wright, Gent., justices. For ₤ 200. 24 July 1744 [sic].
George Byrn is guardian of Wm. Brown, Jno. Brown and George
Brown, orphans.   Geo. Byrn
         Cuthbt. Harrison
 23 July 1744. Ack. and OR.

Pages 512-13. Inventory of the estate of Francis Lacon, dec.,
made in obedience to order of 28 May 1744.
 Includes 4 negroes valued at ₤ 85.
 Total valuation ₤ 120.11.0
 Appraisers sworn before Thos. Harrison, Junr.
         Wm. Thorn
         John Metcalfe
         Lewis Reno
 24 July 1744. Ret. and OR.

Pages 514-16. Inventory of Simon Gosling estate.
 Includes one negro woman valued at ₤ 35.
 No total valuation given.
         Will Adams
         Wm. (W) Foster Sr.
         Thos. (T H) Hart
 Certificate of Wm. Butler that the appraisers were sworn
before him 10 July 1744.
 24 July 1744. Ret. and OR.

Pages 517-18. Estate of Richard Pallister, dec. [₤]
 To paid Mr. Richd. Osborn coroner and constables
  fees 147 lb. Tobo. a 12/6 per Ct.   0.18. 1½
 To pd. Mr. Jeremiah Bronaugh a county and parish
  levy 85½ and a clerks note 22½   0.13. 6
 To pd. Mr. Richd. Osborn per a Judgmt.   1.17. 4
 To pd. Mr. Wm. Dent   9.19.10½
 To pd. Wm. Gladin per Judgmt. 591   3.13.10½
 To pd. Wm. Hale per Judgmt.   3. 3. 4
 To pd. David Dunbar per Judgmt.   2. 9. 7½
 To pd. John Gladin per note of hand 86   0.10. 9
 To pd. part of your rent to John Gladin 200 1. 5. 0
         Lewis Ellzey, admr.
 Contra.
 By Walter Williams   0. 2. 9
 By William Hall   0. 3. 9
 By John Galdin   0. 3. 0
 By Giles Runnals   0.15. 6
 By Thos. Farmer   1. 0. 0

1744

By Mathew Bradly	1.15. 2
By Joseph Debell	1. 6. 3
By John Murphey	0. 7. 6
By William Williams	0. 9. 2
By James Turley	1. 9. 9
By Francis Ellzey	0.17. 4
By Abraham Linzey	1. 4.10
By Gabril Addams Junr.	0.14.11
By William Dowling [?]	0. 5. 6
By Hanner Debell	0.10. 4
By Thos. Williams	0. 5. 6
By John Laswell	0. 7. 0
By John Tramell	0. 2. 6
By Robert Harding	1. 0. 0
By John Feral	0. 5. 6
By Francis Rose	1. 9. 2
By Abell Pearson	0.14. 0
By Jacob Lasswell	2.14. 0
By Lewis Ellzey	1.16. 0

Lewis Ellzey

24 July 1744. Lewis Ellzey exhibited this account which was OR.

Pages 519-20. Bond of William Blackwell, Howson Kenner and Moses Linton, Gent., unto John Wright, John Diskin, Wm. Butler and Benjamin Bullett, Gent., justices. For £ 25. 25 July 1744. Wm. Blackwell and Howson Kenner are admrs. of John Turner.
Wm. Blackwell
Howson Kenner
Moses Linton

25 July 1744. Ack. and OR.

Pages 521-22. Inventory of estate of James Greshon, ordered made 25 June 1744. Appraisers sworn before Capt. John Frogg and Mr. Joseph Hudnall, Gent.
Total valuation £ 88.5.5.
Charles Morgan
Joseph James
Daniel Marr

27 Aug. 1744. Ret. and OR.

Pages 522-23. Bond of Mary Cundiff and Wayman Sinkler unto Joseph Hudnall, Valentine Peyton, John Diskin, William Blackwell, Gent., justices. For £ 50. 27 Aug. 1744. Mary Cundiff is admx. of Isaac Cundiff.
Mary (M) Cundiff
Wayman Sinckler

27 Aug. 1744. Ack. and OR.

Pages 523-25. Inventory of estate of Isaac Cundiff, dec., ordered made 27 Aug. 1744.
Total valuation £ 3.15.11.
James Tebbs
Thos. Arrington
James Muse

20 Sept. 1744. Appraisers sworn before Antho. Seale.
Mary (M) Cundiff signed the inventory.
24 Sept. 1744. Ret. and OR.

Page 525. Isaac Cundiff. Account of estate. 1744.   [L]
  By cash recd. Jno. Diskin   -. 2. 6
  By 50 lb. tobo. Geo. Rogers at 12/6   -. 6. 3
  24 Sept. 1744. Signed by Mary Cundiff.
  24 Sept. 1744. Presented in Court by Mary Cundiff, admx.
of Isaac Cundiff, dec., and adm. to rec.

Pages 525-26. Bond of Cuthbert Harrison and Valentine Peyton
unto Joseph Hudnall, John Wright, Thomas Stribling and
Anthony Seale, Gent., justices. For L 500. 24 Sept. 1744.
Cuthbert Harrison is guardian of Prudence Osborn.
                                              Cuthbert Harrison
                                              Val. Peyton

  24 Sept. 1744. Ack. and OR.

INDEX

Accotink Creek, see Auatinck
Adams, Gabriel 17, 19, 46-47, 117
  John 59
  Richard 59
  (Addams), William 19, 52, 61, 75, 116
Adburn, Thomas 27
Adderton, --- 27
  Jeremiah 68
Addison, William 19, 21
Adie, Hugh 52
Ah Doggarty (Adoughite, A Doughete), Jarvis (Gervase) 100-101
Albin, Thomas 15, 32
Alexander, --- 81
  Gerrard 35, 74, 91
  Jane 35
  Phillip 57
  Robert 35
Allen, George 22
  Jane 22
  John 13, 44-45, 83, 96
  William 16
Allford, Susannah 74
Alliston, Bryant 76
Alphin, William 105
Ambrose, John 110
Amees, --- 69
Anderton, Margaret 38-39
  Richard 38-39, 51, 104
Angel, Charles 85
Arrington, Sarah 47
  Thomas 17, 37, 47, 73, 86, 117
  Wansford 47
Art, Thomas 75
Ash, Francis 99
Ashby (Ashbe, Ashbee), Thomas 1-2, 12, 23
Ashford, Ann will, 6-7
  Constance 6-7
  George 6
  John 5-7, 10, 13, 18
  Mary 6-7
  Michael will, 5-6, 1, 7, 10, 13, 84
  William 6, 84
Ashmore, --- 103
  (Mrs.) --- 44
  John 32
  Mary 23, 31-32, 34, 59

Atwell, Margaret 85
Attwell, Thomas 86
Auatinck Creek 6, 14
Awbrey, --- 12, 20, 69, 89
  (Aubrey), Francis will, 80-82; 5, 12, 16-17, 39-41, 67-68, 74, 84
  George 80-82
  Henry 81-82
  John 41, 74, 80, 82, 84
  Richard 80-82
  Samuel 80-82
  Sarah 80-82
  Thomas 81-82
Ayres, Thomas Acres 82

Backer, Charles 35, 42
Bailey, Elizabeth 116
  (Bayley), John 49, 78
  (Bayley, Baily), William 12, 45, 51, 96
Baker, Charles 50
  William 17, 19, 96
Ball, Edward 87, 92
  James 20
  Sarah 87, 92
Barker, Leonard (Leo, Lee) 4, 8, 19, 24-25, 30, 32, 35, 38, 63, 70-71, 74, 77
  Mary 75
  William 73
Barnett, Thomas 48
Barradel (Barradall), --- 26, 65, 69-70, 88
  Edward 27
Barrister, --- 65
Barry, --- 27
  Edward 4, 11, 31, 44, 47, 54, 56-57, 70, 72, 74, 79, 85, 91, 102
Barton, Anne 48, 53, 57, 60, 75-76
  Valentine 5, 8, 24, 39, 48, 52, 56-57, 59, 75-76
Bates (Betes), Robert 13, 17-19
Battaley (Batteley), --- 20-21, 23, 69, 95, 103
  (Battaile), Mosely (Mosley) 20, 22, 44
Baxter, --- 20
  James 10, 17, 18, 21, 24, 54, 102-104

Baxter, John 30, 59, 75, 79, 97, 103
Bayley, see Bailey
Baylis (Bayliss), William 23, 58-59, 83, 103
Beach, Thomas 79, 88-89
Bean, William 5, 9-10
Beaver damm 52
Becket, Robert 26, 30
Bell, --- 109
  Moses 68, 89
Belt, John 85
Bennett (Bennit), John 85, 87
  (Benitt), Mason 63, 92-93
  Thomas 20
  (Bennit), William 23-24, 29
Bereman, see Berryman
Berkley, William 59
Berry, --- 101
  Henry 105
Berryman (Bereman), Benjamin 15, 62, 78
Betes, see Bates
Bethun, David 53, 55, 70
  Elizabeth 53
  Margaret 53, 79
Bevins, Morris 56
Biding, William 14
Billings (Billing), Jasper 83, 92, 105
Bivens, Mary 1
  Thomas 1
Blackburn, --- 44-45, 77, 83
  R. 70, 99
  Richard 10, 26, 37, 47, 51, 59-61, 64-65, 92, 97, 103-106, 110, 113, 115-116
Blackmore, George 44
Blackwell, Joseph 15, 92, 101, 105, 107-108, 115
  William 15, 20, 80, 92, 99, 101, 108, 110-115, 117
Bland, James 36, 102
  John 104
  Robert 12
  Thomas 92
  William 57-58, 72
Blowers, John 22
Boggess (Bogss), Henry 4, 11, 56
  Robert 65, 77, 88
Bohannan, Joseph 20

Bolling, George 19, 21, 30
  William 18-19, 21, 30
  see also Bowling
Boots, Moses 102
Bosman, Mary 3
  Thomas 3, 5, 66-67, 88-89, 103
Bourke, --- 69
Boutine, Nicholl 44
Bowie, John 22-24, 26, 28, 31-34, 36-43, 46-56, 58, 61-63, 70-73
Bowling, John 31
  see also Bolling
Boyd, George 69
Boystone, John 16, 22
Brabin, (Mrs.) --- 20
  Elizabeth 23-24, 29
Bradford, Daniel 112
  John 20, 108, 111-112
Bradly, Mathew 117
Brent, --- 69, 92
  William 88
Brett, George 104, 106
  Richard 64
Brewster, Hannah 87
  William 38
Bridges, D. 65
  Mary 109
  William will, 109
Bristoe, Thomas 47
Bristol Company 105
Bristow, --- 45
Broadwater, Charles 1, 7, 20-21, 43, 54
  Elizabeth 7, 21, 43
  Guy 20, 42
Bromback, Millkird 4
Bronaugh, --- 27
  (Bronough), David 74
  (Bronough), Francis 74
  (Bronough), Jeremiah 3, 29-30, 33-34, 66-68, 74-75, 79, 88-89, 102, 116
  (Bronough), John 66-68, 74, 88-89, 102
  (Bronough), Samuel will, 74-75; 66-68, 88-89, 102-103
  (Bronough), Thomas 74
Brooke, --- 27
Brooks, --- 66, 70
Brooshaw (Brookshaw), William 17, 19
Broughton, Edward 12, 23

Brown, --   27, 66, 70, 83
   George   116
   Gustavus   61
   James   11
   John   16-17, 41
                  55, 59, 85, 116
   William   116
Bruce, William   19
Bryan, Henry   12
   John   25, 83, 90
Bryant (Bryand), Derby   11-12
Buchanan, Elizabeth   37-39, 42
   George   37
   John   26, 37
   Joseph will 37-38; 39, 42
   Neavill   37
   William   37
Bull, Benjamin   54
Bull run   43-45
Bullett (Bullitt), Benjamin
      12, 23, 40, 42, 70
      95, 98, 100, 105, 117
Bullock, Rachel   52, 83
   Richard   will, 52
                   54, 82-83
   Sarah   52, 80, 83
   Susanna   52
   Thomas   50, 52
                   63, 83, 107
Burdett, John   40
Burn, James   85
   see also Byrn
Burk, James   53
   John   30, 42, 54
Burston, William   53
Bush, John   20, 61
   Thomas   20-21, 25
Butler, William   60, 97
                113, 116-117
Byrn (Burn), George   22, 116
   see also Burn

Caborn (Caborne), Robert
                   23-24, 30
Cale, Elizabeth   98
Calvert (Calvard), George
        8, 25, 37, 45
   see also Colvert
Camell, Margaret   39
Campbell (Camell), Patrick
                      51, 59
Campell, John   25
Camper, see Kemper
Camplin (Champlin), John
        6, 7, 11, 26, 32

Cannady, John   79
Cannon, Duke   44
   Luke   95, 103, 105
Canterbury (Canterberry), John
          44, 45, 61, 113
Carney, Mary   20
Carol, see Carrol
Carpenter, Morgan   12
Carr, John   30-31, 38
                59, 61, 74, 105
Carrol, Eliz.   12
   John   11
   Luke   12
   (Carol) Danel   12
Carter, ---   4, 27, 43
            58, 65, 88, 92
   Edward   89
   Job   3, 77
Carter line   4
Catlett (Catlet), John
                  20, 28, 95
Cave, Benjamin   26, 70
   William   26
Cedar run   43-44
Chambers, Daniel   106
   John   26
Champe (Champ), ---   61, 77
   John   28, 31, 43
                45, 60-61, 78
   William   36-37
Champlin, see Camplin
Champneys, Ann   18
   (Champney), W.   78, 85
   William   12, 18, 24
             53-55, 71, 104
Chandore   4
Chapawamsik Creek, see
   Chopawamsic
Chapman, ---   26
   Elizabeth   23
   John   22
   Joseph will 22-23; 24, 30
   Mary   23
   Nathaniel   20, 59, 103
   Sarah   23-24
   Thomas   34
   Violetta   23
Chilton (Chelton), John
                     107, 111
Chopawamsic Creek   2
Chrystie, ---   26
Chrysty, Robert   69
Claiborn, Nat.   27
   see also Clayborn,
   Clayburne
Clapham, ---   81

Clapham, Mary	32	Coomber, John	98
Clark, Susana	47	Cooper, ---	44
Clayborn, Thomas	11	Elizabeth	14
see also Claiborn		Henry	44
Clayburne, ---	104	John	31
see also Claiborn		Copher, John	90
Clement, Alexander	103	Coram, William	83
Clerks run	81	Corbet, ---	56
Clifton, William	75	Corder, John	108
Coburne, James	44-45	Cork, James	44
Cocke (Cock), ---	21, 27	Cornet, Richard	56
44-45, 66, 69, 76		Cornvile, William	76
87-88, 104-105		Cornwell, Charles	93
(Cock, Cooke), Catesby		Peter	93
5-8, 10-11, 17, 19		Cotten, John	111
22, 26, 30-32		Cotton, Thomas	102
37, 44, 63, 92		Crabb, John	98
95, 102, 104-105		Crandin (Crandon), Honor	13
Coffee, John	83	Creig, ---	83
Coffer (Cofer), Francis		Crooper, see Crupper	
3, 78-79, 102		Crump, John	78, 98
(Cofer), Mary will 78-79		100, 105, 114	
(Cofer), Thomas Withers		Crupper, ---	70
79		(Cruper, Crooper), Richard	
see also Cooffer		19, 22, 59-61	
Cohick	81	71, 79, 83, 104	
see also Pohick (?)		Cullins, James	105
Colcklow, Robert	49	Cummings, Elizabeth	16
Cole, ---	27	Malachi	16
Coleman, ---	20	Thomas	16
Coles, John	27, 61	Cundiff, Isaac	117-118
Collins, see Cullins		Mary	117-118
Colvert (Colvet), Esther		Cuthall, James	99
72, 92			
George	83, 96		
Jane	90	Dacon, see Deaker	
Mary	60	Dagg, James	62-63, 76
see also Calvert		John	94, 107, 115
Colvill, ---	20	Thomas	62-63, 76
(Collvil), John 1, 32, 36		Dalton, Andrew	113
47, 76-77, 103		see also Daulton	
Colvin, John	12	Dargan, Timothy	20
Congrove, Moses	44	Darmont, Catherin	95
Connell, John	72	Darnall, David	96
Simon	72	Jacob	109
Connely, Brian	5	John	114
Conner, Bryan	11	Morgan	101, 110
(Connier), Samuel 15, 23		Darnel, Joseph	83
24, 29, 56-57, 72, 80		Darrell, Sampson	18, 43, 76
Conners, Thomas	85	Daulton, John	101
Conway, Thomas 9, 20, 34, 83		see also Dalton	
Conyers, ---	20	Davey (Davy), William	4, 27
Dennis	103	Davies, (Mrs.) ---	12
Cooffer, John	99	David	77
see also Coffer		Judith	37
Cooke, Elizabeth	26	Richard	12
see also Cocke			

Davies, Thomas	37, 39, 42, 105	Dodson, Ann	87
see also Davis		(Dotson), David	58, 60-61, 87
Davis, John	36, 61	(Dotson), Elisha	58
Joseph	15, 32, 61, 63, 70, 92-93	(Dotson), George	58
		(Dotson), Greenham	58
Margaret	36	(Dotson), Joshua	58
Mary	38-40	(Dotson), Thomas	58, 61, 87
Richard	38, 40		
Thomas	107	Walter	68, 89
William	14, 18, 64, 90, 99	Doggarty, see Ah Doggarty	
		Dogue (Doge) run	6
see also Davies		Dorrets	28
Davison, John	81	Doterty, see Doarterty	
Davy, see Davey		Dotson, see Dodson	
Dawkins, John	49, 51, 59, 61, 86	Doughhete, see Ah Doggarty	
		Douglas, ---	27
Deacin, Richard	33	Dowell, Thomas	96
Deakers (Deaker), Thomas will, 110; 114		Dowling, William	117
		Doyle (Dyal, Droyel), Edward will, 71-72; 4, 73	
Deat, ---	26		
Debell, Hanner	117	Elizabeth	71
John	56	James	71
Joseph	33, 117	(Dyal, Dioyal), Priscilla	71-73, 88
Margaret	33-34, 57		
(Dibiel), William will 33, 34, 43, 57-58		Drakeford (Drakefoot), Anne	72, 76
		(Drakefoot), Elizabeth	72
Debuts, Lawrence	104	(Drakefoot), John	72
Delaney, Joseph	99	(Drakefoot), Mary	72
DeLisle, ---	56	(Drakefoot), Richard will 72-73; 49, 50, 66-68, 72-73, 76, 88-89, 92	
Delisle, Stephen	13, 30-31, 35, 102		
Dent, ---	21, 27, 65		
William	18, 20, 27, 43, 54, 61, 66-67, 102-104, 116	Draper, ---	21
		Droyel, see Doyle	
		Drummond, Aaron	23-24, 30, 40
Deveen, Edward	89	Ben	27
Devin, ---	65	Dulany, ---	21, 54, 69
Dibeil, see Debell		Caven	15, 70, 104
Dickson, James	82, 84	Daniel	66, 88
Digges, ---	66	Dunaway, Catherine	80, 85
William	65	Dunbar, David	116
Dinwiddie, ---	104	Duncan, Elizabeth	42-43, 83
Dioyal, see Doyle		(Dunkan), John	18, 23-24, 42-43, 101, 108-109
Diskin, ---	43-44		
(Diskins), Daniel	45, 51	Joseph	83
John	12-13, 15, 28, 31, 39, 47-48, 52-53, 59, 75, 80, 86-87, 98, 100, 105-106, 108, 115, 117-118	Rice	107
		Robert	83, 99
		Duncom, John	61, 71
		(Duncum, Duncomb), Thomas	61, 71
Dixon, Ann	91		
Doarterty (Doterty), Mary	4-5	Dunlop (Dunlap), William	47, 70
Dodson (Dotson), Abraham	58	Durgin, Timothy	60
(Dotson), Amey	58	Dyle, see Doyle	

Earle, Samuel	15, 63 92, 98, 110
Earp, John	67-68
William	66-68, 88-89
Easter, Giles (Guiles)	will, 75; 76
Jane	75
Edge, John	will, 35-36
Thomas	11
Edwards, John	96, 110, 112
Thomas	83
Eilbeck, ---	27
William	104
Elder, Hundley	46
Jemima	46
Elliot, William	37
Elzey (Ellzey), Francis	117
(Ellzey), Lewis	10, 16-17 24, 29, 31, 48, 33 54, 98, 116-117
Thomas	43, 46
Emms (Embs, Ems), Edward	6-7 10, 20, 42, 77, 88
English, Walter	96
Eskridge, George	21, 23
Estace, J.	1
Evans, John	18, 41, 57, 82
Mary	2
Thomas	83
Ewell, ---	87, 105
Bertrand	97-99, 104-105 107, 113-114
Charles	64-65, 83, 97
see also Youwell	
Exley, Joseph	95
Fairfax, (Farfax) ---	101
Thomas, Lord	59
William	73, 75, 79-80, 82 84, 86-87, 90-91
Falkner, ---	44
Ralph	45
Farguson, see Ferguson	
Farmer, Samuel	45
Thomas	116
Farrow, Abraham (Abram)	will 105-106; 107, 115
Elizabeth	106
Isaac	106
Jane	13
John	13, 15, 61, 106
Lidia	106
Margaret	61, 106
Sibell	106

Farrow, William	30, 32, 35 38, 64, 74, 104, 106
Feagan (Fegan, Feagins, Feagin), Edward	10-11 66-68, 95 105, 108, 115
Francis	115
(Feagin), Henry	115
Feagin (Fegan), Bridget	105, 115
(Fegan), Daniel	115
Fearnley, William	74
Fegan, see Feagan, Feagin	
Felkins, see Filkins	
Feral, John	117
Ferguson (Farguson), Ann	79
Francis	5
(Farguson), Isaac	40, 43
Jane	15
(Fergerson, Farguson, Furguson), John	3, 5 12, 66-67, 70 79, 88-89, 105
Fife, James	77
Filkins (Felkins), Henry	67-69, 89, 93, 99
Rose	92-93
Fishback, Anna Catharina	25
Elizabeth	4, 25
Frederick	5
Harman (Herman)	4, 5, 10
Henry	4, 5, 25
Jacob	5
Jessie	4
John	will, 4; 10
John Frederick	4, 25
John Jacob	4
John Philip	4
Mary	14
Fiter, John Milicpd	will, 14
Mary	14
Fletcher, Aaron	24, 27
James	111, 114-115
John	111
William	24
Fluher, William	11
Fogg, Amos	75
Foot, ---	95
(Foote), George	95-96
Richard	109
Ford, Jane	41
Thomas	1-3, 41, 43 46-47, 49-50
Foster, Conliff and Co.	27
Neal	4, 11
Robert	58

Foster, William	47-49, 58, 61, 77, 87, 116
Fox, Richard	99
Francis, ---	83
Frankham, William	47
Frasher, William	81
Frasur, ---	20
French, ---	104
Daniel	12, 19, 22, 48, 90
Elizabeth	62-63, 100, 106
Hugh	19, 26
James	will 99-100; 45, 61, 95, 101, 103, 106
Mary Ann	100, 106
William	99-101
Frogg, John	63, 80, 83, 101, 107-108, 111, 117
Froom, Elizabeth	81
Peter	81
Frost, James	44
John	18
Fuller, ---	69
Stephen	70
Furguson, see Ferguson	
Furr, Elizabeth	16
Furr, Thomas	will, 16; 20
William	16
Gadds, William	11
Gale, ---	27, 66
Gammerson (Gemmerson, Gommerson), William	67-68
Gardiner, James	34
Garner, Andrew	97, 99
Charles	39
John	39, 98, 107-109, 114
Vincent	107, 110
Gascoigne, Thomas	27, 66, 68, 89
see also Gaskins	
Gash, Joseph	32
Gaskins, Elizabeth	56, 64
Thomas	56, 64
see also Gascoigne	
Gemmerson, see Gammerson	
Gent, George	4-5, 14
Gibb, ---	20
(Gib), James	59, 104
Gibbins (Gibbons), John	107, 114
Rachel	107
Gibson, ---	45
Abraham	7
Ann	7
Gibson, Isaac	7
Jacob	will, 7-8; 1
Jane	8
John	76
Jonathan	16
Gil, James	41
Gist, Anne	75
John	76, 92
Gladin (Gladding), Ann	41
(Gladwin, Glading, Gladden)	
John	17, 29, 33, 58, 77, 116
(Glading), William	75, 116
Glascock, John	36, 42, 50
Peter	36
Glegg, Honor	13
William	will, 13; 15
Glover, Thomas	21
Godfrey, William	1, 4, 11, 55-56, 63, 71, 78-79
Going (Gowin), Alexander	41, 47
(Gowin), John	41, 43, 46-47
Susannah	41, 47
Gommerson, see Gammerson	
Goodall, ---	44
Goodin, George	17
Goodwin, George	18
Goose Creek	4, 80
Goring, George	44
Gosling, Jane	113
(Goslin), John	will 60-61, 14, 71
Mary	60-61
Simon	will, 113, 60, 64, 116
Gowin, see Going	
Graham, Edward	45
(Grayham), James	59
(Grayham), John	26, 47, 52, 76-77, 83, 97, 105-106
Grant, ---	45
(Mrs.) ---	101
Alexander	99
David	4
John	44, 65, 92, 97, 106, 109, 114
Peter	108
Grantham, John	32
Gray, George	44
Thomas	29-30
see also Grey	
Grayham, see Graham	

Grayson, Benjamin 14, 18-19,
      37, 47, 59, 64-65,
      70, 80, 92, 97-99,
      102-104, 106-108, 116
   John   59
Green, Charles   73
Greenhorn, Andrew   81
Gregg, ---   59, 65, 70, 88, 92
   Elizabeth   97
   Jean   97
   John   will 97; 1,
      10, 17, 26, 30, 35,
      37, 44-45, 47, 51,
      58, 64-65, 67, 80,
      95, 97, 99, 102-104
   Mary   97-98
   Mathew   97
   see also Grig, Grigg
Greshon, James will 115; 117
   Mary   115
Grey, John   73
   see also Gray
Griffin, Walter   48
Griffith, (Griffeth, Grifeth)
   Charles   46, 48
   David   84
   (Grifeth), Rebecca   46
Grig, John   102
   see also Gregg
Grigg, (Mrs.) ---   105
Grigsby, ---   26, 69
Grimes, Charles   45
   John   45
   Nicholas   20, 33
Grimsley, Sarah   63
   Thomas   111, 115
Grinnan (Grinan), Owin
                       100-107
Groves, John   85
Guess, Anne   49-50, 62
   Joseph   31, 49, 62
Gunerson, William   89
Gwatkin, Edward   106
   Thomas   113

Habosn, George   98
Hackney, ---   38
   Frances   106
   John   106, 109
   Samuel   76, 96
   William   13, 20,
      22, 35, 42, 54,
      57, 85, 106, 115
Haddox, John   96, 116
   (Haddock, Haddocks), Mary
                         78, 96

Hagan, Edward   34
Hager, Anna Catharina   25
   Henry   will, 25-26; 4, 28
Haggard, James   100
   Margaret   100
Hail, Thomas   85
Hairs, Elizabeth   46
Halbert, Thomas   74
Hale, ---   56
   William 34, 54, 57, 85, 116
Hall, ---   65
   Thomas   103
   William 17, 67, 89, 104, 116
Halley, Henry   97
   James   48
   Thomas   97
Halling, William   84
Hamilton, Henry   13
   Joseph   85
Hamilton Parish, Church-
      wardens   29
Hammel, ---   66, 88
Hampton, ---   65
   Anthony   68
   Hester   46-47, 57, 74
   Joseph   46-47, 57, 74
Hamrick, Patrick   76, 86-87
Hancock, ---   102
   Anne   64-65
   George   114
   (Handcock), John   64, 98
   Scarlet   will, 64; 25,
      31, 70, 78, 88, 104
   William   113-114
Hann, James   31
Hannton, Thomas   70
Harbert, James   38, 42, 85
Hardin, Abigail   9
   Alis   9
   Ann   9
   Elizabeth   9
   George   108
   Henry   8-9
   (Harden), John   1, 8-9, 20
   Mark   will, 8-9
   (Harden), Martin   8-9, 83
   Mary   9
Harding, Robert   117
Hargess, Elizabeth   34
Hargford, John   3
Harl, John   4
Harle (Harl, Harll, Herle),
   William   4, 10,
                     13, 77, 91
Harper, George   107
   John Withers   54
   Samuel   114

Harrell, James	22
Harris, Charles	58
John	85
Harrison, ---	29, 45
Burr	15, 96, 101
Charles	60-61
Cuthbert	96, 98, 101, 116, 118
Edward	108
George	19, 24, 34-35, 43, 47, 54, 103
Margaret	55
Mary	24
Thomas	1-3, 13, 28, 36, 40, 42-43, 48, 50, 94-98, 101, 106, 108, 110, 113, 115-116
Hart, Thomas	52, 76, 116
Harthing, William	19
Hartley, Hannah	85
Hawley, Thomas	11
Hays, George	60
Samuel	85
Hayter, George	81
Heagan (Heagin), Edward	21, 24
Hedges, Robert	3, 56, 111
Hedgman, ---	26
Hegins, Richard	23
see also Higgins	
Helm, Thomas	96
Helms, Leonard	93
Henderson, James	will 31-32, 35, 38, 42
Henry, George	99
Henward (Henwood), John	82
Heryford (Hereford), John	5, 12, 29, 105
Herle, see Harle	
Hewlet, Ambrose	64
Hews, see Hughes	
Hicks, Thomas	73
Higgins, Richard	3, 15, 38-39, 58, 62, 64, 105
see also Hegins	
Higgs, Elizabeth	12
Hill, Thomas	104
Hinson, Walter	88
Hit, Peter	29
Hitt, John	96
Hobson, ---	27
Hoel, ---	26
Hoffman, Agnes	25
Anna Catharina	25
John	4, 25-26
Hogan, Sarah	77
Hogan, Thomas	76, 86
Holbrook, Randall	48
Hollis, John	41
Holmes, Christopher	50-51
Edmund	50-51
James	50-51
John	will, 50-51
Mary	50-51
Holms, Leonard	45
Holtzclaw (Holtsclaw, Holtclaw), Jacob	5, 10, 25-26, 38, 42, 78, 114
John	14, 92
Homs, John	10
Hooper, Thomas	95
Hopper, John	108
Hord, Thomas	18
Hornsby, Leonard	100
Horward, John	59
Hott (Hot), Nimrod	37, 58-59, 80, 86, 91
Housley, ---	51
Howard, James	83
Robert	30
Howel (Howll), Henry	89, 101, 111
Hox, John	20
Hudnall, Joseph	15, 62, 92, 106, 111-112, 114, 117-118
Thomas	will 62-63; 20, 78
William	62
Winney	62-63
Hues, see Hughes	
Hugget, Charles	91
Hughes, Edward	27
(Huse, Hues, Hughs), Ralph	1, 4, 16, 34, 87
(Huse), Robert	60
(Hews, Huse), Sarah	56-57
(Hews, Huse), William	56-57, 63
Hulet, Rosanah	48
Hull, Samuel	81-82
Humphrys, ---	103
Hunger run	4
Hunting creek	6
Hurst, John	59-60
William	70
Huse, see Hughes	
Husk, John	100
Hutchison, Andrew	87
Hutton, Benjamin	31
Hyde, Margaret	46
Hynson, William	65-66

Jacob, Joseph	77	Kemper (Kamper, Camper),	
Jackman, Thomas	19, 31-32, 42	John (Johannes)	5, 25
Jackson, Francis	104		29, 78
Lodowick	80, 83	Kencheloe, see Kincheloe	
Samuel	61, 107	Kendall, Sarah	110
Thomas	38	Thomas	110
James, John	78	William	71, 110, 114
Joseph	117	Kennedy, John	84
Richard	78	Kenner, Howson	52, 92
Janney, Amos	33		97-98, 117
Jarvis, Richard	39, 42	Kent, Isaac	97
	48-49, 61, 73	Kerfoot, Thomas	4
Jenkins, Elizabeth	75, 77	Kerkland, John	92
John	75, 77	see also Kirkland	
Jennings, Augustine	110	Kerr, Peter	43-4
Edmund	66, 68	Kettle Run	8-9
Thomas	20, 57	Key, Philip	87
John, Thomas	84	Kil, Charles	109
John's Branch	50	Kincheloe (Kinchelo, Kenchelo)	
Johnson, ---	46, 65, 69, 88	John	28, 39, 43-45
Christopher	46-47		55, 71, 78-79, 114
Jeffery (Geoggery)	10, 19	King, John	57
	31-32, 35, 38	Samuel	18, 19, 21
	42, 50, 103, 115		32, 67-68, 89
John	1, 2, 23	Kirkland, Richard	103
	66-68, 89, 98, 102	William	56
Mary	13	see also Kerkland, Kirtland	
Susu [Susan?]	40	Kirtland, Richard	51
Jones, ---	26	Kitocton Creek	81
Cornelius	14	Knight, Ephraim	67-68, 89
Elizabeth	14	Knowland, see Nowland	
James	44		
Robert	3-4, 9, 15, 20		
	30, 45, 74, 96-98	Lacon, Francis	will 112-113
	100-102, 104-106		36, 116
	109-111, 113, 116	Jane	112-113
Thomas	13, 114	Lain, James	79
Jordan, Francis	107	Sarah	79
John	107	William	79, 87
Thomas	will, 107-108	Lambath, Sarah	7
	98, 109	Lambert, (Lampers, Lamport),	
Jurdan, see Jordan		Joseph	36-37
		Sarah	36-37
		Lampers, see Lambert	
Keein, see Keene		Lamport, see Lambert	
Keene (Kein), Ann	53	Lard, Owen	36
(Keein), James	55, 72	Lasswell, Jacob	117
(Kein), John	27, 53, 55	Laswell, John	117
	70, 85, 102	Lathem, Stephen	112
(Kein, Keen), Nicholas		Lattimore, John	16
	will 53; 56	Lawson, ---	57, 83
(Kein), Sarah	56	Marmaduke	will 98; 64-65
Kein, see Keene			97, 99, 102
Keirns, Martha	111	Lay, Abraham	20-21
Keith, James	40	Leachman, Thomas	40
Kelly, David	35	Leatherland, James	27, 101

Lee, Henry	87
Lehew (Lehugh), Peter	83, 95
Lewis, John	30
Stephen	12, 15, 69
Thomas	1, 4, 7, 21, 26, 32, 54-55, 103
Vincent	87
Licking Run	4, 25
Lillard, Martha	will, 3; 5
Sarah	3
Linch, William	22
Linsey, Robert	102
see also Linzey	
Linton, Francis	104
John	104
Lettice	80, 104
Margaret	1
Moses	45, 64, 90, 99, 102-104, 113-114, 116-117
William	18, 102-103
Linzey, Abraham	117
see also Linsey	
Littlejohn, Marcellus	3
Mary	3
Lloyd, John	109-110, 115
Lovell, James	104
Low, William	77
Lucas, Ann	34, 38, 59
(Luckus), Francis	34, 38, 43-44, 58
John	91
Luckey Run	50
Ludwell, ---	52
Luis, Thomas	83
see also Lewis	
Luke, ---	65, 88
Luttrell (Lutterall), Simon	34, 107, 115
Lyde, ---	44
Machen, Thomas	108, 115
Mackinley, see McKinly	
Madden (Maden), John	4, 11, 51
Magee, Edward	52
Magier, ---	69
Maguire, Elizabeth	35
Manall, David	101
Manley, John	4, 48, 55, 59
Markham, Elizabeth	1
William	1, 19
Marr, Christopher	111
Daniel	54, 71, 106-109, 111-112, 114, 117
Elizabeth	111
Marr, John	will, 111; 114
Martin, John	102
(Marten, Minster), John	
Joseph	25-26, 29
Joseph	5
* Stephen	38
Mason, ---	11
Ann	10, 27, 33, 69-70, 88-90
French	48
George	10, 12, 26-27, 29, 65, 69-70, 87-89
Mary	10, 69, 87, 90
Thomson	10, 69, 90
Massey, ---	20
Henry	85
Sigismund	90
Mathewis	33
Matthews, Pi	29
William	27
McAntier, Thomas	16
McCan, Timothy	11
McCarty, Daniel	47
Denis (Dennis)	6-11, 13-15, 18-19, 22-24, 26, 28, 31-34, 36, 38-42, 46-49, 51-53, 56, 58, 61-64, 70-72
McClayland, Daniel	106
McColley, Benjamin	94-95
Hester	95
McDonhill, Martha	9
McDoniell (McDoneill), James	8-9
McDowell, Jean	84
Margaret	84
Mary	84
Sarah	84
Thomas	will, 84
McKenny, John	48, 55
McKenzey, Daniel	101
McKinly (McKenly), Margaret	43, 57
(McKenly, Mackinly), Samuel	33, 57
McMillian (McMillion), John	40, 96
Melton, Elizabeth	12
John	56, 73, 82
Richard	12
Mercer, ---	20, 27
John	10, 29-30, 48, 65, 67, 69-70, 76, 87-88, 103
Meryford, John	21
*Martin's Spring Branch	8
Marumsco Creek	64

Metcalfe, John	28, 51, 100, 106, 116	Neale, Presley	91
Middleton, Ann	11	Rodham	will 91; 96, 103
Millard, Richard	52	Neaphwack run	14
Miller, Richard	27, 49	Neavill, George	37-38, 72, 76, 108, 115
Minitree, ---	87-88	John	72
Minor (Minar), John	4, 29, 54, 57	Nelson, Henry	3, 15, 30
		Netherton, Henry	87
Minster, see Martin		Nettle, Mary	111
Minter, Joseph	37-38, 72	Newill (Newel), Benjamin	68, 89
Mobberly, James	82		
Monteeth, Thomas	103	Newport, Peter	96, 107-109, 114
Montgomery, Hugh	105		
Moor, John	100	Newton, Willoughby	76
William	66-68, 88-89	Nichols, William	83
More, Mary	79	Noble, George	11
William	79	Noell, ---	69
Morgan, Charles	52, 54, 82-83, 87, 101, 105, 109, 112, 114, 117	Noland, James	66-68, 88-89
		Pierce (Peirce)	11, 66
		see also Nowland	
Margaret	110	North River	5
Simon	109	North Run of Pohick	71, 78
Morris, Ann	will, 101, 27, 66-68, 70, 89	Nowland (Knowland, Noland),	
		Bridget	11-12
Elizabeth	115	Elizabeth	80-81
James	97	Philip	11, 82
Thomas	115	see also Noland	
Morse, Ebenezer	80, 104	Nutwall, James	53
Moss, Ebenezer	48		
(Mose), Matthew	27, 36, 78, 86		
		Occoquan Creek	97
Moxley, Thomas	85	Oneal, Charles	91
Mountjoy, Thomas	19	Organ (Orgin), Matthew	17-18, 34
Mounts, ---	69		
Mousley, James	19	(Orgain), Solomon	17-18, 30, 33-34, 54
Murfitt, ---	45		
Murphy, Elizabeth	30	Oriar (Orear), Daniel	will 28, 29, 94
Henry	44		
(Murphey), John	30, 75, 117	(Orear), Easter (Hester)	28-29
		John	28-29, 94
William	101	Osborn, ---	18, 27
Murrey, James	15	Ann	39, 55, 77
Muse, James	17, 47, 117	Margaret	39, 55, 77
Musgrove, John	11, 13, 29, 43, 76	Mary	39, 55, 77
		Prudence	118
		Richard	4, 21, 26, 32, 41, 44, 48, 54-55, 59, 62, 75-76, 92, 116
Napier, Rene	63		
Neabsco Creek	60, 105		
Neal, ---	27	Thomas	13, 18, 28, 31, 39, 43, 45, 55, 77-78, 101
Arthur	48		
Neale, Christopher	91, 96	Overall, Behethlan	93
Daniel	91	John	will, 93-94, 42, 50, 95, 96
Elizabeth	39-41		
(Neal), John	39, 41, 82	Mary	93
Lidia	91	Nathaniel	94, 96

Overall, Sarah	93
William	93
Owen, William	51
Owens, John	60
Owsley, Thomas	29
Oxley, Joshua	6-7
Padderson (Pattison), Catherine	will, 41, 43, 45, 47
Pagett, Ruebin	13
Page, Elizabeth	112
Grace	112
Hannah	112
John	will, 112
Sarah	112
William	112
Pallister (Pallaster), Richard	24, 29, 116
Parker, Jonas	68, 89
Mary	7
Sarah	will, 34; 74
Parsons, Sarah	70
Pattison, see Padderson	
Payne (Payn), William	19, 21, 26, 29, 48, 55-57, 59, 62, 76-77, 85
Payton, see Peyton	
Peak, John	103
Peake, William	5, 70-71, 79, 105
Pearson, Abell	117
Thomas	21, 35, 56, 74, 91
Peek, John	48
Perry, William	80
Peyton (Payton), ---	45
Frances	98
John	22
(Payton), Valentine	14, 17-18, 39, 43, 47, 63, 75, 78-79, 89, 91, 97-98, 102, 104-105, 107-108, 116-118
Phillips, Mary	15
Pimmet, George	38
Pinson, Thomas	104
Pohick Creek	14
Pohick, forest of	78
North run of	71, 78
see also Cohick (?)	
Poor, Margaret	76
Pope, Humphrey	39
Potomac River	81
Poultney, Richard	57
Poutney, ---	80
Powell, William	87
Price, Richard	70, 72-73
Pritchet, Christopher	64, 105
Eleanor (Elinor)	85, 91
Puller, William	95
Purcel, John	36
Purnell, Elizabeth	34
Francis	34
John Chapman	25, 34, 74, 107, 115
Quarles, Moses	1
Queen, John	38, 42, 85, 91
Quin, John	11, 23
Rappahannock River	5
great marsh of	74
Razolini, Onorio	69
Reading, Timothy	92
William	92
Reardin, William	102
Rector, Catherine	4
(Rightor, Rickter), John	5, 29, 92, 111
Reeves (Reve, Reeve), John	36, 37, 57, 72
(Reeve), George	57, 72, 77, 87
Regan, Michael	11, 73, 79
William	79, 84
Reid, Joseph	27, 58, 103
Remy, Jacob	59
Reno, John	100
Lewis	94, 116
Thomas	38-39, 95
Rhodry, John	10, 12-13
Ribban, ----	87
Riccia, Elizabeth	56
Richard	56
Richardson, Eliza	55
Jonathan	81
Nicholas	48, 54-55
Rickets, ---	69
Rickter, see Rector	
Ridley, William	113
Rigby, Hugh	21
Rigg, Ann	48
Right, see Wright	
Rightor, see Rector	
Roberts, Mary	53
Richard	81
Robertson, John	2, 3
James	82
Robinson, Margaret	61

Robinson, Thomas 3-7, 10, 13-15, 21, 52
Rock, George 52
Roe, see Wroe
Rogers, George 118
Rookard (Roocard), --- 66-68
   John 60
   Thomas 60
   (Roocard), William 60-61, 71, 89, 113
Rose, Francis 117
Rout, William 19
Royaltie, John 108
Roylte, Elizabeth 9
Runnals, Giles 116
Rush, Benjamin 61
Russell (Russel), Ann 5, 9-10
   Margaret 1, 2, 7
   Nathaniel 1
Rust, Peter 80
Rutter, Richard 17-18

St. Clare (St. Clair), Abraham 27, 65, 71, 103
Sanders, Elinor (Ellionor) will 46; 48
   Mary 46
Sandy (Sande) Run 2
Saunders, Lewis 66-68, 88-89
Savage, --- 66
   Andrew 109
Scandall, Ann 48
Scandret, Pitman 103
Scott, --- 65
   Alexander 20
Scutt, William 20, 41
Seale, Anthony 9, 39, 44, 49, 53, 59, 73, 75, 87, 100, 118
Searson (Seurson), Francis 2, 30, 38, 44, 56
Sebastian, Benjamin 74
Settle, Isaac 83
Shadburn, Jane 10
   John 12, 23
   Mary 10
   (Shadborn), William 10, 12, 23, 94
Shadden, Robert 83
Shepherd (Shephard), Elizabeth will, 53; 55, 70
Sheridan, John 84
Shillon (Shelton?), John 20
Shoemake, John 20
Short, --- 69
   Samuel 26

Shumate, Daniel 9
   Judith 9
Simes (Sims), Mary 73, 76, 86
   (Sims), Richard will, 73, 76, 86
   see also Sims
Simmonds, Thomas 85
Simon, Thomas 9
Simpson, --- 66
   (Simson), Ann 2
   (Simson), Baxter 2
   Gilbert 76
   (Sympson), James 68, 89
   (Simson), Jane 2-3, 15
   (Simson), Richard 1, 18, 43, 46, 48, 55, 63
   (Simson), Thomas will 2-3, 15, 63, 77
   (Simson), William 1-2, 18, 63
Sims, Isbel 111
   James 111
   see also Simes
Simson, see Simpson
Sinclair, Elizabeth 110
Sinkelar, Adam 32
Sinkler, --- 81
   Robert 59, 76
   Wayman 117
Skinker, --- 52
Skinner (Skiner), James 68, 89
Slade, William 43
Sleming, William 48, 55
Smallwood, Bayne 68, 89
Smith, Jacob 9, 49
   John 77
   Mary 19, 22
   Samuel 11-12
   Stephen 111
   Susannah 105, 111
   Thomas 1, 6-7, 10-11, 16-17, 24, 105, 111
   William 19, 22, 97, 108
Sparks, Jeremiah 66-68, 89
   (Sparkes), Mary 11, 13
   (Sparkes), William will, 11; 13, 111
Speak, --- 27
Speere (Spoore), --- 27
Spencer, Frances 91
   James 51
Spicer, Rosser (Rocer) 105, 108
Spiller, Rachel 35-36, 112-113
   William 35, 112

Spore, Ann 104
Spotswood, --- 38
Stace, R. 2
Stan, R. 2
Stark, Susannah 24
   William 94
Staunton, --- 69
Stephen, Robert 40
Stephens, --- 95
   Robert 32
Stephenson, James 111
Stevenson, Mary 25
Steward, William 80, 85
Stewart, Cha. 104
Stone, Esther 37, 56-57
   Francis 56-57, 72, 91
   Thomas 96, 114
   William 66, 96
Storey, James 47
Straughan (Stroughan, Strawn)
   John 21, 41, 57, 74
Strawn, see Straughan
Stribling, Thomas 31, 45
   59, 78, 118
   William 105
Strother, James 22
Stroughn, see Straughan
Sturman, --- 21
   John 4, 15, 17, 29
   39-40, 45, 58
   75, 79, 82, 105
   William 79
Suddath, James 20
Sumners, --- 69
   John 13, 17-19, 21, 77
Sute, Edward will, 40
   42, 50, 94, 95
   Elizabeth 40
   Margaret 40, 94
   Mary 40
Sympson, see Simpson

Tackett, John 113
   (Tackit), Lewis 36, 95
   Mary 36
   William 113
   see also Taquett
Tailer, see Taylor
Tannahill, Matthew 66-68, 88
Taquett, Sarah 113
   see also Tackett
Tarph, John 32, 105
Tasker, Benjamin 34
Tayloe, John 43, 76, 105

Taylor, Charles 35, 42, 45
   49, 57, 76, 78, 96
   George 48
   Henry 43, 48, 68, 88, 105
   John 20
   Mary 49, 57
   Robert 58
Tebbs, Charlotte 86
   Daniel will, 85-86; 98
   Fushee 85-86
   George 85-86
   James 85-87, 98, 117
   William 85-86
Tedwell, Richard 95
Tenant, --- 69
Terrett (Territt, Terret),
   William Henry 35, 54-55
   57-58, 75, 82
Tharton, see Thornton
Thatcher, James 15
   Mary 15
Thomas, --- 27
   David 21
   Mark 85
   Nathan 27
Thompson, --- 26
Thomson, William 70
Thorn, William 28-29
   36, 94, 116
Thornberry, Elizabeth 96, 98
   Richard 96, 98
Thornton (Tharton), Timothy
   36, 78, 86
Tillett, Giles 17-18, 31
   John 1, 18
   Samuel 31
Tilley, Richard 43
Tindall, Joseph 33
Trammel, Daniel 42
   (Tramel, Trammill),
   Gerard 13, 17
   73, 75, 85
   (Tramell), John 42, 46, 117
Traverse, --- 69
Triplet, Thomas 32
Turbervile, C. 9
Turberville, --- 69
Turley, James 117
   (Turly), John 1, 18
   31, 43, 103
Turly, Paul 30
Turner, Edward 20
   James 107
   Jann 7
   John 117
Tuskorora 81

Tyler, ---	44, 69
Benjamin	104
Charles	104, 113
H.	87-88
John	97
Joseph	104
Underwood, Emanuel	43-44
George	2-3
John	2-3
William	70, 72-74
Veal, Bond	59, 104
Elizabeth	60
(Veale), Morris (Maurice)	1-2, 18, 37
(Veale), Rose	109
Vilett (Vilet, Vilot, Violet)	
Edward	46, 62, 66-68, 88-89
Elinor	46
Wade, Zephaniah	46, 82
Wagoner, P.	92-94
Walker, James	25
John	will, 25; 24, 30-31, 35, 103
Robert	25
Wallis (Wallace), Burr	22-23
Jane	22-23
Mary	93, 96
Thomas	93, 96
Walters, Mary	83
Ward, Henry	78
Warsdell, Richard	28
Washington, ---	104
E.	57
Edward	85
Henry	44, 69, 103
Lawrence	47, 83
Waters, Katherine	113
Thomas	45
Watkins, Henry	73
William	73
Watson, Mary	64
Waugh, Joseph	20
Webb, John	12
Welch, Thomas	71, 98
West, ---	45, 69
Hugh	1, 16-17, 20-21, 24, 33-34, 43, 54
John	54, 70
Thomas	26

West, William	15, 29, 44
Westwood, James	61
Wheeler, Richard	41, 57
White, John	116
Whitesides, William	23, 27
Whitfield, ---	43
Whitford, Thomas	17, 19
Whitledge, John	51, 94
Thomas	93, 106
William	42, 50, 94-95
Wiat, Ann	83
James	83
William	83
see also Wyatt	
Wilcocks, John	78
Wilcoxon, John	82, 84
Williams, ---	65
Ann	110
David	98-99, 109
George	81
Hannah	75, 87
James	109
Jonas	will 109-110; 114
Owin	96
Thomas	117
Walter	67-68, 85, 89, 116
William	27, 75, 77, 87, 117
Willis, ---	27, 87
Thomas	55
Wilson, Ann	12
Jacob	80
John	43
Winsor, Christopher	will, 14-15; 16, 29
Sarah	14, 16
Thomas	14
William	14
Wisdell, Richard	12, 23
Wise, John	103
Withers, James	107
John	79
Wood, John	49, 78, 96
Richard	32
Woodcock, Thomas	95
Woodward, Ann	2
(Woodard), Mary	2
Thomas	2
Wren, Thomas	77, 96
Wright, Ann	90
Charles	50
Francis	will, 90; 105
(Right), John	10, 22, 31, 32, 54, 98, 100-101, 106-110, 114-118
(Right), Joseph	35, 42

www.ingramcontent.com/pod-product-compliance
Lightning Source LLC
Chambersburg PA
CBHW030554080526
44585CB00012B/375

Wroe (Roe), William	109	Young, Daniel	49
Wyatt, William	116	Edward will 49; 59, 100	
see also Wiat		John 9, 45, 49, 59, 95	
Wylie, ---	66	Mary 49, 59, 100	
		Thomas 44-45, 58, 65, 69	
		77, 88, 90, 92, 98	
Yoe, Thomas	66		
Youwell, Charles	102		
see also Ewell			